AN IRONIC APPROACH TO THE ABSOLUTE

AN IRONIC APPROACH TO THE ABSOLUTE

Schlegel's Poetic Mysticism

Karolin Mirzakhan

LEXINGTON BOOKS
Lanham • Boulder • New York • London

Published by Lexington Books
An imprint of The Rowman & Littlefield Publishing Group, Inc.
4501 Forbes Boulevard, Suite 200, Lanham, Maryland 20706
www.rowman.com

6 Tinworth Street, London SE11 5AL

Copyright © 2020 by The Rowman & Littlefield Publishing Group, Inc.

All rights reserved. No part of this book may be reproduced in any form or by any electronic or mechanical means, including information storage and retrieval systems, without written permission from the publisher, except by a reviewer who may quote passages in a review.

British Library Cataloguing in Publication Information Available

Library of Congress Cataloging-in-Publication Data Available

ISBN: 978-1-4985-7891-2 (cloth)
ISBN: 978-1-4985-7893-6 (pbk)
ISBN: 978-1-4985-7892-9 (electronic

CONTENTS

Acknowledgments	vii
Introduction: Paradox and Philosophizing Together	xi
1 An Ironic Approach	1
2 To Be Ironic Is Divine: Hegel's Aesthetics and the Threat of Irony	35
3 Another Way to the Absolute: Language and Naming in the *Dao De Jing*	59
4 How to Read a River: Poetic Mysticism in John Ashbery's *Flow Chart*	87
Bibliography	111
Index	115
About the Author	119

ACKNOWLEDGMENTS

The early German romantics emphasized that the philosopher is not a solitary thinker, but rather that she is part of a community of her peers—poets, scientists, and writers—who share in the sacred activity of philosophizing together, or *symphilosophie*. This activity happens in the bond between the writer and the reader and it is described by Schlegel as a philosophical friendship, both within one's self and with others. I am grateful to those members of my community who supported and encouraged me throughout the process of writing this book.

I am thankful to my mentors who have consistently supported my questions and writing from the earliest stages into the present day. Elizabeth Millán Brusslan introduced me to Schlegel's fragments and has resolutely supported my intellectual endeavors ever since. Kevin Thompson has been an indispensable mentor and guide. His insistence that I consider "Meno's paradox" on every early draft of this work has informed the themes that run throughout it. Franklin Perkins introduced me to non-Western philosophy and in particular to the *Dao De Jing*—this text has remained with me and informed my writing and teaching. María Acosta has been an enduring and enthusiastic supporter of my work and a generous critic. Without the influence of Peter Wake, I probably would not be writing on German philosophy, for better or for worse; in his classes, as an undergraduate, my love for philosophy was awakened. I am also thankful to Jeffrey Reid for reading early versions of this project and providing critical feedback that informed this book. I am grateful to Ian Moore for engaging in the conversations about Schlegel's fragments that would serve as the basis for this interpretation. I am extremely grateful to Jana Hodges-Kluck at Lexington Books for her enthusiastic support of this project and her patience as it has developed, as well as to my anonymous reader whose comments and questions pushed me toward clearer articulations of my ideas.

I am fortunate enough to have dear friends and colleagues who were willing to read drafts of these chapters: Anahita Vieira edited drafts on her busiest days. Her attention to detail, care, and thoughtfulness as a writer and scientist are reflected in this book. My friendship with Robert Puccinelli informs the stories throughout this book. The fourth chapter would not exist if he had not introduced me to John Ashbery's *Flow Chart*. Katie Homan's poetic writing inspired me as I worked through her generous feedback. In addition to engaging in dialogues with me about irony and reading parts of this work, Zack Sievers created the beautiful image that appears on the cover.

I am very lucky to have had an enormous community of friends and a strong support network while I was working on this project: the lobsters (Robert Puccinelli, David Shuey, Cayenne Sullivan, Jennifer Fett, Pablo Garcia Seiquer), Brook Celeste, Carol Robinson, Jenn Kutsch, Dorcas Beasnael, Jessica Elkayam, Kevin O'Neill, Candice Hall, Deanna Giolas, Nicole Van Pelt, James Hannigan, Carl Hill-Popper, Nadia Sawicki, and Boomer Trujillo. I am grateful for the community of writers in Atlanta with whom I shared many silent hours as I completed this book.

Cynthia Lindner and Geoff Ashmun: It is hard to convey in words the immense and positive impact that you both had on my life and my writing. Thank you for pushing me, encouraging me, and believing in my capacities.

To my students at DePaul University and Kennesaw State University: Your keen ability to decipher Schlegel's ironic texts proves that he was right when he said there would be a future reader that would know how to read him. You are those readers and I am grateful for your hard work grappling with many of these texts. Your insights influenced me and are reflected throughout this book.

I had the opportunity to present parts of this work at the *Comparative and Continental Philosophy Circle* (CCPC). I am grateful that such a venue exists where philosophers are encouraged to pursue comparisons with non-Western philosophy and where generous conversations about that work can happen. In particular, I'm grateful to Franklin Perkins for encouraging me to write comparatively and present at the CCPC and to my colleague at Kennesaw State, David Jones, for supporting comparative philosophy in general and my writing in particular. I am also grateful to the University of Minnesota Press for allowing me to reprint materials from Peter Firchow's translation of *Friedrich Schlegel's Lucinde and the Fragments* (1971 by University of Minnesota), to Ferdinand Schöningh for generously allowing me to reprint materials from the *Kritische Friedrich Schlegel Ausgabe* (*Zweiter Band*), as well as Georges Borchardt, Inc., and Carcanet Press for granting me permission to reprint lines from *Flow Chart* by John Ashbery (Copyright 1991 by John Ashbery; Reprinted by permission of Georges Borchardt, Inc., on behalf of the author; All rights reserved).

I am thankful to my family—my mother Josephine, my father Sam, my brother Stephan, and my grandmother "Nanny"—for helping to instill in me an inquisitive nature that would lead to my pursuit of philosophy, for the freedom to follow those questions, and for my love of language and communication.

And, of course, my dog Bhikku, who patiently waited (and napped) while I edited each draft.

This list cannot capture the many influences that helped shape this project, nor can it convey the sacredness of the bond through which the lofty task of *symphilosophie* is accomplished.

INTRODUCTION

Paradox and Philosophizing Together

I begin our investigation of Friedrich Schlegel's romantic philosophy, and the role of irony therein, with a sojourn into Plato's *Meno*. In the dialogue, Socrates and Meno discuss the nature of virtue and whether it can be taught or is acquired in some other way. Socrates exhorts Meno—who has given many fine speeches on the matter—to define virtue. Meno initially answers confidently, but, after several failed attempts to satisfy Socrates, he gives up and, in exasperation, accuses Socrates of being a "broad torpedo fish" that has made his mind and tongue numb. Socrates is willing to accept this characterization if Meno agrees that Socrates is also numb. In other words, if Socrates has confused Meno and left him numb, it is only because he is also perplexed as to the nature of virtue. Nonetheless, Socrates tells Meno that he would welcome the opportunity to continue searching together for a definition. At this point in the dialogue, Socrates (and the reader) are presented with a paradox by Meno: How can you search for something if you do not know what it is? And, if, by chance or in some other way, you encountered it, how would you even know that you had? In other words, searching for what we already know is futile, and searching for what we do not know is impossible.[1]

I have chosen to begin this exploration of an ironic approach to the Absolute with a Socratic dialogue for a few reasons. First, Schlegel will inaugurate his transformation of irony in its philosophical homeland

and with Socrates. As readers of this Socratic dialogue, our interpretation of the text will hinge on whether we maintain that Socrates' statements are ironic and, if we do, which definition of irony we ascribe to when we make this judgment. Secondly, the conception of the Absolute for Schlegel, which I will expound throughout, struggles against Meno's paradox; in brief, how can we strive to know the Absolute if we do not know what it is that we are searching for? Even if we were to come into contact with it, how would we know that we had? Third, Socrates' invitation to search for the definition of virtue *with* Meno is an example of Schlegel's concept of *symphilosophie*, as doing philosophy with the other, or philosophizing together. Indeed, the relationship between a reader and a writer is an ideal space for successfully executing *symphilosophie*. The writer guided by the goal of *symphilosophie* is the synthetic writer who designs her reader and brings her forth.[2] The synthetic writer engages with her reader as still "alive and critical," rather than already fully formed.[3] Because she must create her reader, the synthetic writer faces a delay—she will not be understood until such a reader exists. Worse yet, her writing may fail to create an audience who understands her.[4] In contrast, the analytic writer simply observes the reader as she already is and produces a text that will maximize the appropriate impression upon that reader. As I will elaborate throughout, Schlegel is a synthetic writer whose primary means for enacting *symphilosophie* is irony. As a synthetic writer, Schlegel leaves room for his reader to affect the text's meaning; however, by saying less and by writing ironically, Schlegel risks being misunderstood by his reader.

EARLY GERMAN ROMANTICISM

Friedrich Schlegel is considered by scholars to be the leading thinker of the early German romantic movement [*Frühromantik*], as well as a foremost thinker of irony. *Frühromantik* lasted from approximately 1794 to 1808 in Jena and Berlin. The *Athenaeum* journal, published from 1798 to1800, was a major venue for the development of romantic philosophy during this period. The *Athenaeum* emerged out of a close group of friends now referred to as the early German romantics (an anachronism since this group of friends never referred to themselves as "romantics").[5] This close-knit group of friends that became the contributors to the journal included August Wilhelm and Friedrich Schlegel (the initiators of the journal), Caroline Schlegel, Dorothea Veit, Friedrich von Hardenberg (Novalis), Ludwig Tieck, and Friedrich Schleiermacher.[6]

Several characteristics distinguish the early German romantics from their predecessors. First, they emphasize that philosophy is an infinite activity rather than a final product in the form of a completed system (belonging to its creator). The activity of philosophizing does not begin with a self-sufficient first principle upon which it would be possible to build toward a conclusion regarding the nature of reality or the Absolute. For the romantics, philosophizing begins *in media res* (or "in the midst of things") and progressively works toward a better understanding of the matter at hand.[7] However, as I will argue, particularly through the intervention of Daoism, the ideal of linear progress will be disrupted by the notion of the Absolute that emerges in Schlegel's philosophy, as well as by the non-linear and non-totalizing method of approaching the Absolute offered by the ironic fragments.

Second, the early German romantics not only stress the incompleteness of all systems of human knowing, but they also claim that philosophy itself is incomplete. Philosophy has gotten as far as it can on its own; it must be united with poetry and science.[8] The philosopher, in the romantic model, is a poet-scientist-philosopher. This mixing of disciplines will alter each component: Poetry will become scientific, science will become poetic, and philosophy will become a scientific-poetic endeavor, in both its content and form. Not only are the disciplines joined together, but the philosopher is also not a solitary thinker; in the romantic circle, the activity of philosophizing is a communal effort. Schlegel emphasizes this communal aspect of philosophy to his readers when he writes that the phrase "my philosophy" is as absurd as the utterance "my God," as if God or philosophy could belong to any one person.[9]

Third, in this model for philosophizing that enjoins us to collaborate, the fragment and the dialogue are the privileged forms for philosophical engagement. Philosophy is a dialogue between different thinkers spanning time and place, as well as between the myriad disciplines. As a form, the fragment also highlights the role of dialogue; the term "fragment" already implies separation from a larger whole, or from other fragments. Like the thinkers and disciplines, the fragments are also in conversation with one another.

Finally, the infinite striving that characterizes romantic philosophy is motivated by the desire to know the Absolute. Novalis describes this yearning in his first Pollen fragment when he writes, "We *seek* the absolute [*das Unbedingte*] everywhere and only ever *find* things [*nur Dinge*]."[10] To rephrase Novalis' concern in terms of Meno's paradox: How can we look for the Absolute (the unconditioned) if all we are ever presented with are things (subject to conditions for their arising)? In this text, I will define the Absolute tentatively as the whole, or that which is unconditioned. I will elaborate this tentative definition in chapter 1; however, an important aspect of the Absolute as the whole, or as oneness, is its non-relationality. As the unconditioned, the Absolute is not connected to a cause (or condition) for its arising. Insofar as the Absolute is the whole, it must contain all relationships within itself and it cannot be in relation to anything else that would limit it. Therefore, if we seek to know the Absolute, as oneness, we abandon oneness as soon as we conceive of ourselves as separate from that which we seek to know. Our usual ways of knowing separate the "I" from what it seeks to know, and therefore forms of poetic expression, such as the literary technique irony, are necessary in order to communicate the whole without cutting it apart by separating the knower from what she seeks to know. If the knower is separate from the whole, then the whole is not truly a oneness, but rather it has already become a twoness (as I will elaborate in chapter 3, on Daoism). Poetic techniques, particularly irony, facilitate the reader's intuition of the whole as whole. Certain poetic techniques allow for an intuition of the Absolute as a unity, without splitting it apart. Ironically, for the romantics, the fragment is the form for the intuition of the whole. Through their form, the fragments proclaim their incompleteness, and in so doing, they leave room for that which necessarily exceeds them.

Throughout this text, the language being used to describe the philosophical striving to know the Absolute will betray the very methods that the writers in question wield; terms such as "closer" or "nearer," which are used to describe a striving "toward" the Absolute, emphasize a linear, rather than a cyclical, model for philosophizing. To say that the Absolute "contains" oppositions turns it into a thing, an imagined container, which is separate from its contents; this expression turns the unthinged into a thing. The romantics do not begin *"in media res"* because they lack the rigor to seek first principles, but rather because this beginning point expresses the nature of the Absolute as non-relational. The Absolute includes the poet-knower. As poet John Ashbery puts it, we are in a "gluey embrace";[11] philosophy's task, through irony, is to reveal that we are already in this embrace.

POETIC MYSTICISM

During the early German romantic period, a new conception of a dynamic Absolute emerges from Schlegel's philosophical fragments. This book will focus on irony as a primary technique for realizing the Absolute in Schlegel's *symphilosophical* project. I use the term "poetic mysticism" to describe the experience of realizing the Absolute, which can be traced back to particular texts. These texts are mystical in nature; I retain the term "mysticism" to refer to an intuition of the whole that is non-discursive and that has its own temporality—of flashes. I qualify this mysticism as "poetic" insofar as the intuition of the whole is tied to particular texts that initiate it. It is not possible to give a fully rational, systematic account of how this experience is generated because the primary technique employed is irony, and irony can never be fully comprehended and articulated without turning the ironic utterance into an unironic, direct expression. However, this does not mean that poetic mysticism is entirely indemonstrable. Rather, it is possible to give an account of the techniques used by certain poetic texts to facilitate an encounter with the Absolute in communion with their readers. The techniques that perform romantic striving will themselves be unironically described in the chapters that follow. Moreover, all attempts to capture the work of irony will always be undercut by irony itself; thus, no complete account can ever be given of how precisely irony makes possible an intuition of the whole.

Although I am arguing for a conception of the Absolute that is at odds with dominant interpretations,[12] I preserve this term in my arguments, because it tethers the reader to a central concept for philosophers during the nineteenth century (unlike the term "Dao," which might be more appropriate). As such, I will retain the term "Absolute" as a subterfuge operating throughout this book, as a way of naming that which cannot be named—a necessary deception to aid the reader, a name that points to the limitation of all names.

CHAPTER SUMMARIES

In chapter 1, I examine the development and genesis of irony in order to understand how Schlegelian irony, or irony as the "form of paradox," alters its traditional meanings. I argue that Schlegel's development of irony lays bare aspects of the traditional definitions, which were previously only implicit. I will argue that irony is a primary technique through which the striving to know the Absolute is enacted in Schlegel's romantic philosophy. Irony cultivates the agility of mind needed for the reader to intuit the whole. Here, Meno's paradox re-emerges in a different form: if irony cultivates the appropriate stance in the reader, how will the reader know whether she has arrived at the necessary disposition for intuiting the Absolute?

In chapter 1, I argue that Schlegel transforms the meaning of irony and that irony plays a central role in his romantic philosophy. In the subsequent chapters, I engage this definition of irony in dialogue with three interlocuters: G. W. F. Hegel, John Ashbery, and the ancient Daoist text the *Dao De Jing* (or *Laozi*). Each conversation partner will bring to light a different aspect of Schlegel's romantic philosophy, especially as it pertains to the role of irony and to the textual nature of the striving for the Absolute. This book will take seriously the romantic commitment to philosophy as an activity of synthesis, rather than separation or limitation, by bringing Schlegel's romantic philosophy into conversation with both ancient and contemporary texts. Chapters 3 and 4 are an application of the romantic imperative to join philosophy with poetry. The *Dao De Jing* and *Flow Chart* succeed in bringing their reader in contact with the Absolute through poetic mysticism.

Chapter 2 takes up Schlegel's ironic project against the backdrop of G. W. F. Hegel's criticism. Hegel's characterization of irony points to the legitimate dangers of the creative and destructive potential of an unlimited or absolute ego. For Hegel, the ironic genius is the individual who regards only what she creates (and thus is capable of destroying) to be substantial; there is nothing that she considers to be real, independent of her creations. I will respond to Hegel's critique in order to illuminate certain elements of Schlegel's philosophy, particularly his emphasis on self-restraint. Restraint appears in both the form and content of Schlegel's philosophical project. He writes in concise, self-contained fragments, and the content of the fragments repeatedly emphasizes the importance of self-restraint for the writer and knower. Moreover, restraint is not merely self-restraint; the writer is also limited by language, by irony, and by the audience with whom she is in conversation.

Chapter 3 focuses on the site of emptiness or incomprehensibility in Schlegel's fragmentary writings through a comparison with the ancient Chinese text the *Dao De Jing*. These texts are co-illuminating: Both emphasize the role of that which cannot be known and exceeds the realm of the human, but which is necessary for knowing to happen at all. This chapter deals explicitly with the issue of language that runs throughout the book, such as how attempts to communicate the Absolute inevitably betray what they seek to name. The *Dao De Jing* offers resources for poetic language that expresses the Absolute without mastering or objectifying it; its presentation of the *Dao* emphasizes a conception of the Absolute that is dynamic and generative. In order to describe the *Dao*, the text appeals to metaphors, which underscore the role of emptiness in the utility of natural and artificial objects. Additionally, and crucially, the text performs the emptiness it describes in its many metaphors at the level of its form: It remains mysterious and cryptic through its use of paradox. The *Dao De Jing's* emptiness thwarts its reader's typical relationship of mastery toward texts and thereby conveys absoluteness as a dynamic movement.

Chapter 4 is a reflection on John Ashbery's poem *Flow Chart*. I argue that the poem's movement can be read as ironic in the Schlegelian sense. This book-length poem contains no apparent narrative; its movements resemble waves, which approach and break apart from meaning before the reader. Ashbery is a writer who welcomes contingency and outside influences into his poetry. Because Ashbery introduces the element of chance into his writing process, a text emerges that is not under the complete control of its author, and which cannot be fully grasped by its reader. The text's autonomy—its resistance to definition—enables it to perform absoluteness.

NOTES

1. Plato, *Meno*, trans. G. M. A. Grube, 2nd ed. (Hackett Publishing Company, 1980).
2. References to the fragments are cited according to their number and abbreviated as follows: AF = Athenaeum Fragment, CF = Critical [Lyceum] Fragment, I = Ideas. References in the original German are from Friedrich Schlegel, *Kritische Friedrich-Schlegel-Ausgabe*, ed. Ernst Behler, Jean Jacques Anstett, and Hans Eichner (München: F. Schöningh, 1958–). Translations are from Friedrich Schlegel, *Friedrich Schlegel's Lucinde and the Fragments*, trans. and ed. Peter Firchow (Minneapolis: University of Minnesota Press, 1971).
3. Schlegel, *Lucinde and the Fragments*, 156–157. KFSA II, p. 161, CF 112.
4. Indeed, both Socrates and Schlegel were misunderstood by their contemporaries. The theme of misunderstanding will reappear in chapter 2 where I discuss Hegel's sharp criticism of Schlegel. In part, Hegel's critique stems from his need to distinguish the destructive capacity of irony from the high place of comedy (and, in particular, Aristophanes) in his system of the fine arts. Whereas Hegel's exemplar of comedy is Aristophanes, Schlegel's ancient Greek reference point for irony is Socrates; it is not incidental, especially with the difference between the synthetic and analytic writers in mind, that Socrates was sentenced to death by the Athenians, whereas Aristophanes never received more than a slap on the wrist as punishment for the content of his comedies.
5. Philippe Lacoue-Labarthe and Jean-Luc Nancy, *The Literary Absolute: The Theory of Literature in German Romanticism*, trans. Philip Barnard and Cheryl Lester (Albany: State University of New York Press, 1988), 6.
6. Elizabeth Millán-Zaibert, *Friedrich Schlegel and the Emergence of Romantic Philosophy* (Albany, NY: State University of New York Press, 2007), 12.
7. Schlegel, *Lucinde and the Fragments*, 171. KFSA II, p. 178, AF 84. "Subjective betrachetet, fängt die Philosophie doch immer in der Mitte an, wie das epische Gedicht."
8. Schlegel, *Lucinde and the Fragments*, 251, I 108.
9. Ibid., 173. KFSA II, p. 180, AF 99
10. Novalis, *Philosophical Writings*, trans. Margaret Mahoney Stoljar (Albany: State University of New York Press, 1997), 23.
11. John Ashbery, *Flow Chart: A Poem*, 1st ed. (New York: Knopf, 1991), 26.
12. In *The Romantic Absolute*, Dalia Nassar details the metaphysical and epistemological interpretations of the Absolute that have come to dominate

scholarship on the romantics. On one side, Manfred Frank reads the Absolute as merely an epistemological notion, much like the Kantian regulative ideal. On the other side, Frederick Beiser understands the Absolute as a metaphysical idea in line with Spinoza's substance. Nassar's thesis is that these two sides need to be thought in a notion of the Absolute that unites both the epistemological and metaphysical view in order to provide an account of not only "what" the Absolute is, but also how we gain access to "it." For Nassar, this access is possible through a "special mode of thought" that is "nondiscursive" or "nonconceptual." In other words, on Nassar's reading, Schlegel's position is that we can grasp the Absolute through intellectual intuition, i.e., an intuition that grasps the whole as a whole. Nassar argues that intellectual intuition has the advantage that it does not objectify the Absolute. Dalia Nassar, *The Romantic Absolute: Being and Knowing in Early German Romantic Philosophy, 1795–1804* (London and Chicago: University of Chicago Press, 2013), 5–6, 108.

I

AN IRONIC APPROACH

Friedrich Schlegel is considered one of the central philosophers of the early German romantic movement and a foremost thinker of irony. In this chapter, I will argue that the romantic striving for the Absolute, a core feature of romantic philosophy, is enacted, in Schlegel's fragmentary writings, by irony. The irony of Schlegel's fragments should not be conceived of as independent from or in tension with his romantic project, but rather as integral to it. My intention, in joining poles of interpretation that favor romantic striving over irony, or vice versa, is pedagogical in nature. That is, my aim is to teach the reader how to interpret the irony of the texts, with the recognition that no complete account of irony can ever be provided, for it is irony that disrupts our attempts at closure.

Schlegel provides one of his clearest definitions of irony in Critical fragment 48, where he defines it as the "form of paradox."[1] In order to unpack this definition of irony and to locate irony's place in Schlegel's romantic philosophy, I will first briefly sketch an operative definition of the Absolute. Then, I will chart some of the terrain regarding how irony has been traditionally understood, as well as how scholars conceive of Schlegel's development of the term. Next, I will put forth my own interpretation of how Schlegel shifts irony's meaning in Critical fragment 48 and provide some examples of fragments that illustrate his use of the term. Finally, I will join Schlegelian irony with the ideal of romantic poetry in order to argue that irony is the means for achieving this ideal.

THE ABSOLUTE

Although a yearning for the Absolute is an essential quality of romantic philosophy, Schlegel does not explicitly define the Absolute. The Absolute cannot be communicated directly by way of a definition that would capture all of its qualities or enumerate all of its predicates. Throughout this text, I will treat the term "Absolute" as synonymous with the whole or the unconditioned; I refer to its meaning as borrowed from the Latin *absolutus*—as non-relational, non-relative, or not dependent. Put positively, the Absolute is free from all dependency; it is absolved of all conditions. As non-relational, the Absolute can be conceived as that which contains all relations within itself but is not in relation with anything else. As non-relational, the Absolute is not dependent on a cause for its becoming; it does not have a condition for its arising; it is the unconditioned [*das Unbedingte*]. The Absolute is not a thing; but rather the name for the dynamic whole, which is the unity of both being and non-being.

When, out of the need to communicate, we employ names such as the "whole" or the "Absolute," we set the Absolute apart from what it is not, and therefore turn what is non-relational into a thing in relationship with other things. Naming automatically creates a split between the name and what it refers to, or the signifier and signified; as soon as I say "Absolute," I take oneness and turn it into a twoness. I make the Absolute into something it is not: something two. This split also applies to the relationship between the Absolute and the knower; as soon as "I" attempt to know or communicate the Absolute, the Absolute is placed into a relationship with the knower and the whole is fragmented. Moreover, the name "Absolute" makes it seem as if there is a thing, the Absolute, which is distinct from all other things—a thing among things. Naming objectifies the Absolute. Irony is a form of indirect communication that does not fall prey to the deficiencies of other linguistic conceptualizations. Ironically, by presenting us with two or more meanings, it allows an intuition into the whole without splitting it. I will return to the problem with naming in the ancient Daoist context; there, I will explore a notion of a dynamic Absolute, which contains all relationships within itself, but which is not a container that is separate from these relations. Additionally, Daoist texts provide rich resources for how language can skillfully communicate the Absolute without, at the same time, turning it into what it is not. For Schlegel, this skillful mode of communication is irony.

IRONY'S FORMS AND IRONY AS THE FORM OF PARADOX

The development and genesis of irony begins, appropriately enough, in its homeland: philosophy.[2] Describing Socratic irony in Critical fragment 108, Schlegel writes that it is "the only involuntary and yet completely deliberate dissimulation" in which "everything should be playful and serious, guilelessly open and deeply hidden."[3] If Socratic irony deceives its listener, then it does so in an entirely voluntary and involuntary manner. This description of Socratic irony is a departure from the operative meaning of *eironeia* for the ancient Greeks. After elaborating possible interpretations of Schlegelian irony, including *eironeia*, I will return to this fragment in order to argue that Schlegel's appeal to Socratic irony operates as a subterfuge for his own definition of irony as the "form of paradox."

In "Masks of Negation: Greek Eironeia and Schlegel's Ironie," Eric Miller traces the meanings of the *eiron* in fifth and fourth century BCE Attic Greek in order to argue that Schlegel consciously resuscitates the meaning of this term with a new motivation.[4] Citing uses of the term from Aristophanes, Plato, and Aristotle, Miller claims that, in general, *eironeia* names the "disingenuous self-deprecation, in which the *eiron* makes some aspect of himself, be it virtues or be it worldly goods, seem less or worse than it actually is."[5] In the comedies of Aristophanes, the *eiron* is the liar, the charlatan, or the cheat.[6] According to this definition of *eironeia*, Plato's Socrates is the *eiron* who understates his position; for example, in the dialogue referred to in the introduction, the *Meno*, Socrates tells Meno that he doesn't know what virtue is, but that he is still eager to continue the search for a definition with Meno. But, if he doesn't possess knowledge, how could he be so sure all of Meno's responses are wrong? According to this ancient Greek definition of the *eiron*, Socrates understates his own position in order to further some end; in this case, the end could be the inquiry into the matter at hand, or perhaps, the desire to make Meno aware of his own arrogance on the topic of virtue. In Aristotle's *Nicomachean Ethics*, irony appears within the taxonomy of the virtues; each virtue is a mean between two extremes (or vices). When discussing the virtue of truthfulness, Aristotle provides its deficiency and excess; both are vices related to truth-telling. The excess of truthfulness is boasting or overstating one's position; the deficiency of truth-telling is *eironeia*. The vice (as a deficiency) related to truth-telling is not, as one might suspect, dishonesty, but rather it is irony defined as understating one's position.[7]

When Schlegel defines irony as "Socratic irony," Miller argues that Schlegel is resuscitating the ancient Greek meaning, but with a new "higher-order" motivation. Miller focuses his account on irony's role in artistic activity, which has three components for Schlegel: self-creation [*Selbstschöpfung*], self-destruction [*Selbstvernichtung*], and self-restriction [*Selbstbeschränkung*]. I will discuss some fragments in which Schlegel elaborates the connection between these three forces in chapter 2; in brief, artistic activity relies on creation, the destruction of what has been created, as well as the limitation of both the creative and destructive urges through restraint. Miller argues that *Selbstbeschränkung*, self-limitation or self-restriction, appears as negation, because the artist seems to be destroying her creative effort by putting limits on it or by pointing out its limits.[8] However, through appearing to weaken her own creative effort by identifying its limits or flaws, the artist can "create the contradictions that will actually make her artwork infinitely greater" and capable of indirectly expressing "[the] deep, infinite meaning that cannot be expressed directly."[9] The self-critical work contains contradictions and therefore expresses more than a straightforward artwork could. Limitation qua critique appears as an external force acting upon the artist's creation (as a negation of it), but it is merely the appearance of negation, which remains under the artist's control all along. The artist maintains her sovereignty, because she is the one introducing the element of limitation in order to produce a final product that is infinitely richer due to the fact that it contains its critique within it. Miller equates the moment of self-limitation [*Selbstbeschränkung*] with irony as the force that "can control the two contradictory moments," most notably the moments of self-destruction and self-creation involved in the artistic process.[10] Miller is critical of interpretations of irony that would remove the author's and reader's autonomy (such as Paul de Man's, which I will address shortly); he argues that irony, as a force of limitation, only appears as a negation, but is really always under the control of the artist who wishes to convey "infinite meaning."[11]

Whereas the ancient Greek definition of *eironeia* entails dissimulation, often carried out for personal gain, Miller argues that Schlegel resuscitates this meaning so that any dissimulation is no longer for mere personal gain, but for a "higher-order" aim, i.e., the "dialectical, positive-creative movement that he can gain from the appearance of negation."[12] Irony facilitates a self-critical work that can express infinitely richer meaning, because it acts as a force that can hold contradictory moments together. However, the definition of irony that most readers will have in mind as they approach Schlegel's text is neither the ancient Greek sense of *eironeia* nor Schlegel's resuscitation (on Miller's analysis), but rather the traditional rhetorical definition that survived the Middle Ages.[13] With respect to the rhetorical definition, irony is a "figure of speech by which one wants to convey the opposite of what one says."[14] For example, I say, "Isn't this weather beautiful?" but you infer from my tone or the context (e.g., a thunderstorm) that I really mean the opposite of what I say. Although the speaker does not mean what she literally says, in some predictable way, she communicates, to her listener, that she means the opposite. To put it differently, I say "A" but you infer from my tone or the context that I really mean "not A."[15]

In a related sense of irony, the speaker does not communicate the opposite of what she says, but rather uses the term "irony" to express that an event or outcome was the opposite of what was intended or anticipated. For example, "Ironically, her attempts to keep close relationships in her life, ended up pushing everyone away." Or, "When making argument X, the author actually produces the outcome they intended to avoid." For example, the skeptic produces a dogmatic position as a result of her argument.[16] In these cases, a situation is ironic because the opposite of the intended result (of an action or line of argumentation) was produced, usually against the agent's intentions.

If, in the ironic statement, the speaker or writer does not mean what she says in earnest, but instead she intends a meaning that is the opposite of what she says, then the ironic utterance is dependent upon distance from the subject matter at hand. With this requisite distance, irony gives its user license to take on any position at will. This form of irony is not limited to speech acts only: I could dress ironically, walk ironically, or enjoy films, television and music ironically. Distance will be the central feature of Hegel's characterization of Schlegel as a divine ironic genius who considers himself exempt from laws and morals. Hegel's critique will be the focus of chapter 2.

Paul de Man picks up on the turn away from the literal meaning conveyed in the rhetorical definition of irony in order to argue that irony's role, as this turning away, is purely disruptive. In his 1977 lecture "The Concept of Irony," which ironically uses the term "concept" in its title, de Man attempts to provide a definition for irony, a difficult task, he claims, since irony is not at all a concept; if irony were a concept, it would be possible to venture a definition, i.e., to directly communicate its meaning.[17] Paul de Man argues against attempts to diffuse irony's power by reducing it to a mere aesthetic device [*Kunstmittel*], i.e., a device that achieves "a playful aesthetic distance, in relation to what is being said."[18] He argues that scholars have tried to weaken irony's force either by reducing it to an aesthetic device or by attempting to understand irony's function; however, he claims, to the contrary, that irony cannot be understood insofar as it is "always of understanding."[19] Irony is tied to whether understanding is possible and therefore cannot itself be understood; we cannot point to whether or not a text is ironic, because it is precisely irony that disrupts our attempts at understanding. Irony is the trope of all tropes, because it names the turning away from meaning that all tropes perform.[20] In other words, de Man is arguing that a trope is a pattern of words, such as a metaphor or allegory, which marks the deviation from a literal to a figurative meaning, and irony names this "turning away" that all tropes achieve.[21] If irony refers to the very turning away from meaning, then it is impossible to understand irony insofar as all our accounts of irony will be interrupted by it.

To support his claim that irony is the trope of all tropes, de Man refers to an unpublished 1797 fragment from "Zur Philosophie." In the fragment in question, Schlegel writes, *Die Ironie ist eine permanente Parekbase.*"[22] De Man translates this phrase as irony is a "permanent parabasis."[23] Parabasis is the interruption of discourse or of a narrative line by a shift in the rhetorical register.[24] In Attic comedy, the parabasis occurs when the chorus steps out onto the proscenium and directly addresses the audience in the author's name.[25] For example, in the revised (and only surviving) version of Aristophanes' *Clouds*, the chorus addresses the audience during a parabasis in order to scold them for their bad taste, since the original version had lost the competition at the

Greater Dionysia. A parabasis, in writing, is a shift in the rhetorical register, which operates like an anacoluthon. Paul de Man cites the example of an anacoluthon in the lies of Albertine in Marcel Proust's *Recherche*: "He says she begins a sentence in the first person, and so you expect that what she's telling you—they're dreadful things—she's telling you about herself, but by some device in the middle of the sentence, without your knowing it, suddenly she's not talking about herself anymore but about that other person."[26] De Man claims this syntactical interruption functions exactly like a parabasis, i.e., it "interrupts the narrative line."[27] As a parabasis, irony interrupts narratives; irony is disruptive. By claiming that irony is a "permanent parabasis," Schlegel, on de Man's reading, is not claiming that parabasis occurs at one point in a narrative, but rather at all points. Irony is a turning away from meaning, a trope, that interrupts all narratives of meaning, permanently, at all points in the narrative. As permanent parabasis, irony not only disrupts narratives, but, de Man argues further, all theories of the narrative. Irony's function as a permanent interruption cannot be contained within any narrative structure that it interrupts—as in the example from Proust—or by any theory that would attempt to fix its meaning.

In "Understanding Irony: Three *Essais* on Friedrich Schlegel," Georgia Albert claims that, as parabasis, irony achieves the interruption of fiction by reality, but also the infiltration of reality by fiction (because the interruption of the "fictional illusion" is performed by a parabasis, which purports to be reality but is also merely fiction). Albert concludes that this means that we are "always already a character in the play" and even our self-awareness that we are a character is part of the play.[28] By disrupting the narrative structure of the play with reality, a parabasis points out that the play is merely a play, and simultaneously points out that the parabasis is also a fiction—like our self-reflection that we are in a play.

A permanent parabasis is (almost) unthinkable; it is, according to de Man, "violently paradoxical."[29] It is an interruption (by its nature, temporary), which occurs permanently. De Man's reading of irony is a compelling interpretation of irony outside of the romantic context; however, its emphasis on the disruption of all system-making and on the impossibility of any narrative is at odds with a central tenet of romantic philosophy, i.e., the striving to know the Absolute. Furthermore, the description of irony as "permanent parabasis" can be regarded as an iteration of the definition of irony as the "form of paradox." Schlegel is challenging his reader to consider an interruption that is permanent, defying the very essence of what makes it an interruption. I think de Man is right that this is a paradoxical thought, but I would claim, against de Man, that Schlegel harnesses the power of paradox, through irony, to bring his reader into contact with the Absolute. I will elaborate this claim in the following section.

With some of the terrain necessary for understanding the development of irony sketched briefly above, I now return to the definition of Socratic irony in Critical fragment 108 in order to propose my interpretation of Schlegel's transformation of the term. When Schlegel invokes Socrates as the model for irony, he alters the meaning of the Greek *eiron*. Socrates, on Schlegel's account, is no longer the *eiron* as the interlocuter who feigns ignorance, often for personal gain. As he says, in the same Critical fragment, Socratic irony "is meant to deceive no one except those who consider it a deception."[30] Irony is no longer merely a form of dissimulation, nor is it a means for the speaker to misrepresent herself. Irony is not a mere rhetorical device through which the speaker says one thing but means another. Irony, through Schlegel's re-articulation, is no longer deception or pretense, but rather, as he says in Critical fragment 48, it is the "form of paradox." Through its form, irony allows the positing of contradictory claims. Fittingly, Schlegel's characterization of irony contains qualities that are opposites of one another: It is, at once, open and hidden, playful and serious, intentional and involuntary. With this transformation of irony, the speaker or writer no longer means one thing but says another; rather, in earnest she posits two equally true statements, which contradict each other. Irony is the form that allows the paradox to hold without collapsing: The propositions in the ironic statement do not conflate into one another, and neither proposition is permitted to subsume the other. One of my students described irony's function using metaphors from architecture: Irony is the structure that preserves the paradox. The metaphor is instructive but limited, because irony is a structure that is, strictly speaking, no-thing.

Schlegel's definition of irony, as the form of paradox, alters both the ancient Greek and the traditional rhetorical definitions insofar as it makes explicit what was merely implicit in those earlier forms. To unpack this claim a bit further: In the rhetorical form of irony, the speaker says one thing (A) but means another (not-A); broken down, an ironic statement includes both what the speaker says and what she means (or what is left unsaid); thus, the form of the traditional ironic statement is the coincidence of what is said and what remains unsaid. What is said and what is not said are opposites, which are joined together in the ironic statement. Irony brings together presence (the statement as literally uttered) and non-presence (what remains unspoken). As the form of paradox, irony names the force that makes possible the holding of a contradiction; however, in Schlegel's re-articulation the speaker "intends" both statements. Irony already did this work of holding together opposites, at least implicitly. Schlegel's definition makes what was implicit in the workings of irony explicit. As in the earlier simplistic example of the weather, I now mean both that the weather is beautiful (A) and that it is not beautiful (not-A). However, the unsaid is not limited to one meaning; as unsaid, it is the site of unlimited potentiality. Writing about the speculative quality of the poetic statement in general, and not irony in particular, Gadamer expresses this relationship between the said and the unsaid beautifully when he writes in *Truth and Method*, "To make oneself understood, means to hold what is said together with an infinity of what is not said in the unity of one meaning and to ensure that it be understood this way."[31] However, with irony, as I will continue to elaborate, the speaker cannot ensure that she will be understood.

Schlegel appeals to Socrates to describe a form of irony that is not a mere dissimulation or rhetorical device, but rather the revival of irony in an earnest form—an earnest irony. If irony no longer refers to the linguistic act in which the speaker or writer says one thing but means another, and if it now refers to the act of meaning both terms as equally true, then in one sense it is paradoxical because the reader or listener is at an impasse; she cannot simply choose one claim or the other. This feeling of being stuck is the same as Meno's paradox: If I can neither search for what I know or what I do not know, then I cannot search. However, my contention is not that Schlegel employs irony in order to show his reader that she cannot know the Absolute and that therefore it is not worth continuing her striving; rather, he is more like Socrates in that he wants to continue searching with his interlocutor. Schlegel's writes ironically as a means for enacting this search with his reader. Furthermore, the realization of our limitation or inability to achieve complete comprehension brings us nearer to knowing the Absolute.

Meno's realization that he could not provide a definition for virtue was a necessary part of the path toward knowing. Or, as Schlegel's friend and fellow romantic, Novalis, puts it in his *Romantic Encyclopedia*, "Error is the necessary instrument of truth."[32]

By expressing what is stated and what is not, or "A" and "not-A," the ironic utterance brings us in contact with absoluteness, or the whole which must contain oppositions. However, unlike the rhetorical definition of irony, there is no longer an implied agreement at the level of language whereby the listener knows, as a consequence of particular modifications in tone or through context, that the speaker means the opposite of what she literally says. In Schlegelian irony, the speaker intends both meanings at once; if the reader only takes one of the meanings to be true (i.e., either the spoken or the unspoken), then communication is only partial, and the ironic fragment fails.

IRONY AS THE FORM OF PARADOX IN THE FRAGMENTS

Next, I examine several fragments in which Schlegel's definition of irony as the "form of paradox" is apparent. These fragments force the reader to consider contradictory claims and, as a result, they bring her into contact with the Absolute, which must contain oppositions and the space that allows those oppositions to emerge. Irony presents its interlocutor with a violation to the principle of noncontradiction and in so doing communicates the whole, which contains contradictions at the ontological level (being and non-being, presence and absence), as well as the semantic level (positive and negative formulations of a proposition).

For example, in *Athenaeum* fragment 77, Schlegel writes,

> A dialogue is a chain or garland of fragments. An exchange of letters is a dialogue on a larger scale, and memoirs constitute a system of fragments. But as yet no genre exists that is fragmentary in both form and content, simultaneously completely subjective and individual, and completely objective and like a necessary part in a system of all the sciences.[33]

Schlegel explains that while there are already genres that are fragmentary in their respective forms, there is no genre that is fragmentary in both its form and content, i.e., "completely subjective and individual, and completely objective." But, how is it possible for a genre to be both completely subjective and completely objective? How can a genre be completely self-standing and, at the same time, the necessary part of a system? Rather than providing his reader with the blueprint for a new type of genre, Schlegel propels her into mid-air; she's unable to land on one side of the dichotomy of subjective/objective or part/whole. As readers of Schlegel's fragments, we are forced to suspend, however momentarily, traditional dichotomous thinking, which operates through simplistic oppositions. Schlegel thwarts his reader's attempt to fully *comprehend* this fragment through fixing and ossifying its meaning into simple, one-sided categories. As a fragment ostensibly about different fragmentary genres, it suspends its reader's ability to neatly categorize the fragmentary genre as either subjective or objective. At the same time, this fragment, amongst others, accomplishes the creation of a new genre, which Schlegel is describing within it. The *Athenaeum* fragments are simultaneously individuals, which can be read and understood on their own, and parts of the whole collection.

Schlegel continues his description of the fragment in *Athenaeum* 206, "[A] fragment, like a miniature work of art, has to be entirely isolated from the surrounding world and be complete in itself like a [hedgehog]."[34] Schlegel writes that a fragment must be "entirely isolated"; however, by using the term "fragment," he is, by definition, indicating that what he is describing has been broken off or separated from a larger whole; the fragment is always a fragment of the whole. This fragment implicitly contains a contradictory claim: the fragment is entirely independent and isolated, but also part of a whole from which it originates. Describing the "logic of the hedgehog" in *The Literary Absolute*, Lacoue-Labarthe and Nancy write, "[each] fragment stands for itself and for that from which it is detached."[35] Schlegel echoes this explanation of the part-whole relationship in Critical fragment 14 when he writes, "[in] poetry too every whole can be a part and every part really a whole."[36] In other places, Schlegel describes the parts of the poem as free citizens, each with the right to vote.[37] Like the parts of the poem, the fragment is a whole of its own, but one that reflects the greater whole. Take the culinary example of a cookie crumb: each crumb is a reflection of the larger whole of the cookie (through its ingredients, texture, or flavor). The fragments too reflect the whole.

Each fragment performs absoluteness in its structure (and in particular through its irony). Even though the crumbs are a reflection of the whole cookie and the fragments are a reflection of the larger whole to which they belong, no combination or aggregate of fragments or crumbs can achieve a return to the whole.[38] Furthermore, separation from the whole is part of the structure of the fragments, which is not to be overcome; rather, the fragment is precisely the mode through which the Absolute can be communicated.

Describing a cultivated work in *Athenaeum* fragment 297, Schlegel writes that "[a] work is cultivated when it is everywhere sharply delimited, but within those limits limitless and inexhaustible; when it is completely faithful to itself, entirely homogenous, and nonetheless exalted above itself."[39] Paradoxically, a work is cultivated (perhaps also like the cultivated person) when it is limited and self-contained, and, at the same time, limitless and reaching beyond itself. Schlegel is not merely forcing his reader to consider the finite alongside the infinite, but, I would argue, he is positing two senses of the infinite in one and the same fragment as his description of the work of art. In *The Infinite*, A. W. Moore outlines two clusters of concepts that have dominated the way the infinite has been understood historically.[40] On the one hand, there is the notion of the mathematical infinite, which is generally characterized in negative terms: inexhaustibility, boundlessness, unlimitedness, endlessness [*unendlichkeit*], and immeasurability. The infinite is greater than any assignable quantity, i.e., given any determinate part, there is always more to come. This cluster of concepts emphasizes potentiality and tends to inform mathematical and logical discussions of infinite.

On the other hand, there is a sense of the infinite that informs metaphysical and theological discussions.[41] There, the infinite is defined by employing positive terms, which emphasize actuality: wholeness, completeness, unity, universality, absoluteness, perfection, self-sufficiency, and autonomy. The first cluster of concepts carries with it the sense of incompleteness, whereas the second, in sharp distinction, carries the sense of actual completion. What is paradoxical about the work of art is that it presents both senses of the infinite—the mathematical and the metaphysical—at once. It is autonomous, self-sufficient, and complete, i.e., those qualities characteristic of the metaphysical sense of the infinite. At the same time, its meaning is inexhaustible, endless; it is mathematically infinite. The artwork is sharply delimited, bounded, and, at the same time, it is boundless, limitless. In this fragment, Schlegel is speaking ironically, insofar as his operative definition of irony is that irony is the "form of paradox." To describe the work of art is to speak in paradoxes in order to get at what it is. The work of art presents, simultaneously and immediately, both senses of the infinite. Furthermore, the two senses of the infinite are connected through irony. Irony produces the metaphysical sense of the infinite as the form that allows for the coincidence of opposites. And, by thwarting our attempts to fix the work's meaning, irony yields its inexhaustibility (or the mathematical sense of the infinite).

Describing systematicity ironically, Schlegel writes in *Athenaeum* fragment 53, "It is equally fatal for the mind to have a system and to have none. It will simply have to decide to combine the two."[42] That is, Frederick Beiser explains, it is fatal to have a system insofar as that system would set arbitrary limits on the inquiry at hand and it is fatal to not have a system at all since unity and coherence are essential to knowledge.[43] The mind must have the agility to think systematically while resisting the impulse to close the system, or to have the last word. This capacity is strengthened through the mind's engagement with ironic texts, and it is not the same, I contend, as Beiser's conclusion that what remains once a decision is made to both have a system and have no system is "the persistent *striving* for one."[44] Beiser's claim implicitly prioritizes the system as a regulative ideal toward which knowers endlessly strive, rather than equally maintaining both options, as Schlegel does in the ironic fragment.

Repeating the themes found in his characterization of Socratic irony, Schlegel writes in Critical fragment 23 that the "good poem" is "wholly intentional" and "wholly instinctive."[45] The good poem is described through the coincidence of opposites—as intentional and instinctive—but what does it mean to be *entirely* intentional and, at the same time, *entirely* instinctive? To borrow the phrase from Ricarda Huch, the fragments are "hard-shelled nuts"; she explains that "[without] the reader's energetic intellectual engagement they are totally incomprehensible."[46] The experience of engaging with Schlegel's fragments as "hard-shelled nuts" can be compared to the role of koans in Zen Buddhism; koans are riddles that the Zen master provides to his students.[47] They are not meant to be comprehended, but rather it is when the student stops trying to comprehend them that she can experience a flash of realization. The Absolute is not approximated through mere aggregation; it is not possible to simply add more predicates until the whole is reached; rather, the experience of intuiting the whole is akin to the moment of sudden realization that occurs after trying to understand the koan and then realizing the mere understanding cannot do this work. Through repeated exposure to the fragments, the reader builds up a tolerance for irony; her mind becomes agile and she is able to approach the Absolute. The student-teacher (or author-reader) relationship just described implies that the teacher is further down the path or has at least experienced flashes of insight. However, to be further down the path ought to be understood in a cyclical sense. In the Zen tradition, advancing means returning to beginner's mind, i.e., to a mind that is vast and spacious and that has yet to split its subject matter apart from itself. Beginner's mind can also apply to the ironic philosopher; after all, Socrates is wise because he is the one who knows that he does not know.

AN IRONIC TREATISE ON IRONY: "ON INCOMPREHENSIBILITY"

Perhaps the strongest example of irony in Schlegel's early romantic writings is his short essay "On Incomprehensibility" ["Über die Unverständlichkeit"]. This essay was published in 1800 in the final issue of the *Athenaeum* journal as a response to criticisms launched at the fragments for being incomprehensible. Schlegel begins the essay "right at the spot where the shoe actually hurts" and cites one of the *Athenaeum* fragments, which was attacked by a critic. He quotes *Athenaeum* fragment 216, which states, "The French Revolution, Fichte's *Wissenschaftslehre*, and Goethe's *Meister* are the greatest tendencies [*Tendenzen*] of the age."[48] Schlegel begins his defense of this particular fragment by first stating that it did not even contain any irony and should not have been misunderstood.[49] In *Irony and the Discourse of Modernity*, Ernst Behler provides justification for an unironic interpretation of this fragment. There, Behler claims that the late eighteenth century saw at least three revolutions: in politics, in philosophy, and in literature. On this interpretation, Schlegel's fragment is merely an inventory of these three revolutions.[50]

After initially claiming that fragment 216 did not contain any irony at all, Schlegel proceeds to explain what he meant by the word "tendency," since the irony of the fragment (and thus the source of its misunderstanding) could perhaps be traced to the multiple meanings of this term.[51] First, he could have meant tendency as a "temporary venture" that would be completed by himself or someone else. Or, he could have intended tendency to mean a venture that was incomplete insofar as it did not include its own starting point; in this latter sense, he would be using this term to describe how he had placed himself on Fichte's shoulders just as Fichte had placed himself on Reinhold's and so on leading all the way back to the "prime shoulder." In an ironic twist, the meaning of the term "tendency" has doubled: incomplete can mean unfinished, as in to be completed by someone else; or, incomplete can mean relying on someone or something else for a starting point. The essay as a whole is also a tendency in this double sense: 1) It does not begin with a first principle or foundational claim, but rather it commences in *"in media res,"* i.e., in the historical present in which Schlegel is being confronted with negative reviews of his fragments; and 2) it does not work toward a decisive conclusion in the form of a final interpretation on the meaning of the ironic fragments.

After dissecting the double meaning of tendency, Schlegel abruptly declares, letting "irony go to the winds," that he meant that "everything now is only a tendency," and we are living in the "Age of Tendencies"; however, he leaves it up to the reader's wisdom to decide whether or not these tendencies will be corrected at all and by whom. By leaving this judgment to the wisdom of his reader, Schlegel is underscoring the inexhaustibility of the text: Its meaning is never complete, and it remains unfinished because it is open to new interpretations rendered by its future readers. Recall that, the cultivated work is the one that is both complete unto itself and completely open-ended; however, this does not entail that all texts have infinite meanings;[52] in the case of "On Incomprehensibility," its inexhaustibility is the result of its irony (as I will continue to elaborate).

Foreshadowing what will be the structure of the essay as a whole, Schlegel first claims that fragment 216 was not ironic at all; then, he claims that perhaps the word "tendency" was the source of the misunderstanding and attempts to parse out its double meaning for the reader; finally, he admits to the irony throughout the *Athenaeum* fragments, but he does not provide the reader with a definitive interpretation of this, or any other, fragment. Schlegel's analysis of fragment 216 forecasts the structure of the whole essay, and, in so doing, it trains the reader of the essay by preparing her for its irony.[53] Since Schlegel initially asserts that fragment 216 is unironic and then later states that it is indeed ironic, this means that any of the fragments could be equally regarded as ironic and as unironic; and, at the meta-textual level, this means that this very essay about the incomprehensibility of the ironic fragments could also be ironic. Again, Schlegel is providing useful instructions to his reader: in any of its moments, this essay that she is reading can be interpreted as ironic or unironic.

Although Schlegel begins "On Incomprehensibility" with a gesture toward resolving the misunderstandings of his critics, he swiftly changes his tone; he no longer attempts to clarify the misunderstandings of the *Athenaeum* fragments by dividing up their ironic and unironic moments. Rather, he states boldly that the "incomprehensibility of the *Athenaeum* is unquestionably due to the *irony* that to a greater or lesser extent is to be found everywhere in it."[54] Citing his own Critical fragments 108 and 48 in which he provides a definition of irony in terms of Socratic irony as "the only involuntary and yet completely deliberate dissimulation" and irony as the "form of paradox," Schlegel begins to defend the irony of the fragments; he calls irony "daily fare" and he expounds an entire system of irony, which he models on a poem by the French poet Chevalier de Boufflers about the types of hearts: "Grands, petits, minces, gros, médiocres, énormes."[55] Schlegel's ironic system of irony begins with the most rudimentary type of irony and works its way up to the "irony of irony." This system will include each type of irony discussed earlier: the ancient Greek definition of *eironeia*, the rhetorical definition, and parabasis. At the base of all these forms of irony, Schlegel includes irony as the "form of paradox." To build a system of irony is itself an ironic gesture, since it is irony that disrupts our attempts to produce complete systematic accounts.

"Coarse irony" is Schlegel's term for the most rudimentary irony that courses through the nature of things and determines their structure. This irony, as the "form of paradox," is encountered in the ancient Chinese symbol *yinyang* (as I will discuss in chapter 3), wherein *yin* (darkness) and *yang* (light) are the two opposing but complementary forces that make up the universe. Coarse irony can be also observed in the structure of crystals; as Elaine Miller has pointed out, the romantics were fond of crystals, perhaps, in part, because their organic structure includes both splitting and unity.[56] As the system advances from the coarsest irony to its subtler forms, the next two types in the taxonomy are "fine and extra fine irony." The latter, extra fine, consists in insulting someone without their being aware of it; this is the irony of the ancient Greek definition, and it is found in the liars and charlatans of Aristophanic comedy.[57] Dramatic irony, the next type of irony in the system, is similar to the concept of a parabasis or anacoluthon, i.e., it is marked by a shift or interruption in the narrative structure. Schlegel explains that this sudden shift in the storyline occurs because the author has become a new person in the fourth act. Double irony indicates two simultaneous meanings; in the context of the theater, there is one meaning for the gallery and one for the boxes.[58] At the height of this "system" of irony is the "irony of irony," which occurs

> [for] example, if one speaks of irony without using it, as I have just done; if one speaks of irony ironically without in the process being aware of having fallen into a far more noticeable irony; if one can't disentangle oneself from irony anymore, as seems to be happening in this essay on incomprehensibility.[59]

By including the "irony of irony" in the system, Schlegel is informing his reader of the ironic operation underway. Schlegel is explaining the meaning of irony while also performing it; as it progresses, the system of irony becomes a self-reflection on what is happening to Schlegel as he is writing. It is Schlegel who can no longer disentangle himself from the irony of this essay. This is another moment in the essay where Schlegel is training a future reader who would no longer regard the fragments as incomprehensible, i.e., as he says, a reader who would know how to read. As a synthetic and ironic writer, Schlegel cannot depend on already having an audience who understands him. There is a delay in comprehensibility with irony because Schlegel must create his reader; he must teach his audience how to read the irony of the fragments. If he fails in this task, he risks being misunderstood. Insofar as the fragments were misunderstood by their critics, "On Incomprehensibility" serves as another opportunity to train (or re-train) the readers of the fragments.

Toward the end of the short essay, Schlegel admits that his fragments were written in the "heat of irony," that irony is the "form of paradox," and thus he essentially confesses that the doubling of meanings is the very source for the misunderstanding. Any effort to unpack, simplify, to clarify, or untangle the irony would do violence to it and betray his project. Moreover, irony is not an incidental stylistic choice made on Schlegel's part, but rather it is the literary technique that cultivates the agility of mind necessary for his reader to consider two opposing claims at once. And, it is through this agility that the reader is brought in contact with the Absolute. This agility can be compared to the ability to see both the duck and the rabbit in the famous image employed by Wittgenstein in his *Philosophical Investigations*. It is nearly impossible to see both images at once—an individual may first see a duck, then a rabbit, or vice versa; but the more agile her mind, the more quickly it will be able to move between the two images, until a near simultaneity is achieved.

Immediately following his claim that he cannot take back the irony in the fragments, Schlegel asks his reader:

> But is incomprehensibility really something so unmitigatedly contemptible and evil? Methinks the salvation of families and nations rests upon it. If I am not wholly deceived, then states and systems, the most artificial products of man, are often so artificial that one simply can't admire the wisdom of their creator enough. Only an incredibly minute quantity of it suffices: as long as its truth and purity remain inviolate and no blasphemous rationality dares approach its sacred confines. Yes, even man's most precious possession, his own inner happiness, depends in the last analysis, as anybody can easily verify, on some such point of strength that must be left in the dark, but that nonetheless shores up and supports the whole burden and would crumble the moment one subjected it to rational analysis. Verily, it would fare badly with you if, as you demand, the whole world were ever to become wholly comprehensible in earnest. And isn't this entire unending world constructed by the understanding out of incomprehensibility or chaos?[60]

In this passage, Schlegel claims that states, systems, and even happiness are the "artificial products of man" [*Die künstlichen Werke der Menschen*] and that these products are created out of "incomprehensibility or chaos." Schlegel is claiming that incomprehensibility or chaos lies at the "base" of these various systems and thus it is not prudent to attempt to make everything comprehensible [*verständlich*]. That is, there is something at the "base" of the system that "must be left in the dark" otherwise the whole system will crumble.[61] Schlegel warns us against trying to understand everything, because, in our attempts at complete comprehension, we risk destroying the very thing we wish to know.

Although "incomprehensibility" and "chaos" are grouped together at the end of the passage, they have two different valences. Incomprehensibility can be corrected or overcome, at least in part; that is, what is incomprehensible can become comprehensible (either through clarifying the text, removing the irony, or producing a new kind of reader). Chaos, however, does not permit progressive or incremental movement toward comprehension. Chaos names the absence of order; that is, to invoke the term "chaos" is to point to an outside of comprehension or understanding, which is not merely the result of a poor articulation or an easily correctible misunderstanding.

Throughout the quoted passage from "On Incomprehensibility," Schlegel warns his readers to be careful when subjecting the greatest human creations to the scrutiny of reason. However, the moments in the English translation where the quote references "rational analysis" or "blasphemous rationality" [*frevelnder Verstand*] are better translated from the German "Verstand" as the English "understanding." In her article, "Friedrich Schlegel, Romanticism, and the Re-enchantment of Nature," Alison Stone draws on Critical fragment 104 to argue that, for Schlegel, the understanding is a peculiar form that rationality assumes when it operates independently of nature; understanding is a species of rationality, which "divides and *analyses* whatever it studies."[62] Although Schlegel does not use the term understanding [*Verstand*] in Critical fragment 104, he distinguishes two types of reason [*Vernunft*]. The first is what normally gets called reason, but is the thin, watered-down type and is only a "subspecies" of reason. This type matches what Stone refers to as the understanding as a species of reason that "divides and *analyses*." Schlegel distinguishes this first type of reason from the "thick, fiery kind" [*eine dicke feurige Vernunft*], which "makes wit witty, and gives an elasticity and electricity to a solid style."[63] This fragment suggests that there is a type of rationality that does not merely dismember reality or analyze by dividing, but rather energizes our pursuits by acting as a coagulant. This means that, for Schlegel, rationality is more far-reaching than understanding, and hence when, in "On Incomprehensibility," Schlegel warns his readers about the danger of excessively applying rationality, he is warning them against overusing that thin, watered-down form of rationality, i.e., the understanding [*Verstand*], which breaks things apart in order to make them comprehensible [*verständlich*].

To make the world fully comprehensible is to be able to encompass it or to make it fit into the structures of human knowledge. Schlegel compliments those artistic creations of human beings, namely all the structures of meaning, but he points our attention to what lies "outside" those structures and cannot be grasped by them. Because the structures of meaning are created by the understanding out of incomprehensibility or chaos, this means that if we scrutinize them intently enough, we will reach "something" not comprehensible, which nonetheless serves as the "basis" for those structures. Although I have used the terms "something," "outside," and "basis" in this analysis, that which does not lie within our attempts at system-making is not, strictly speaking, a thing, nor is it spatially outside. What Schlegel is attempting to convey to his reader is that the understanding creates systems out of chaos, and thus chaos is both a source and a limit point for what we can know.[64] Schlegel links chaos to creation in *Ideas* fragment 71 when he says that confusion [*die Verworrenheit*] is only chaos when it gives rise to new worlds.[65] What exceeds comprehension is both the impetus for the systems that the understanding constructs, as well as their limit point. What exceeds human knowing is not anything, but the no-thing that allows for the possibility of discourse. In this sense, "it" does not occupy a particular space out beyond systems, but rather the space of no-space, or of non-presence, that paradoxically allows for the generation of presence. It is, strictly speaking, not knowable, and our attempts to know it discursively will fail.

Rather than attempting to comprehend the world, Schlegel instructs his readers to cultivate versatility of mind. In *Ideas* fragment 55, Schlegel writes, "Versatility [*Vielseitigkeit*] consists not just in a comprehensive system but also in a feeling [*Sinn*] for the chaos outside the system, like man's feeling [*Sinn*] for something beyond man."[66] A universal or many-sided approach is not achieved by merely creating a more comprehensive system, but rather by having a sense for what lies outside of our attempts at system making, or by having a feeling for that which lies outside the realm of the human. This versatility of mind, or agility, is cultivated through the irony of Schlegel's fragments. Reiterating the connection between chaos and irony, Schlegel writes in *Ideas* fragment 69 that "[irony] is the clear consciousness of eternal agility, of an infinitely teeming chaos."[67] Irony cultivates a mind that is agile enough to have a sense for that which it cannot know, but which limits its pursuits. By urging the reader to consider two opposing statements at once, irony develops mind that is multifaceted and capable of thinking systematically while resisting the urge to complete the system, to have the last word, or to achieve absolute knowing.

Thus far, I have taken Schlegel's warning about the excessive application of the understanding literally. However, insofar as the essay remains thoroughly ironic, this statement ought to be read in at least two ways. Schlegel declares that we (philosophers in the Age of Criticism) should to be careful in how we apply the understanding, but at the same time, and in that very same paragraph, he is giving an explanation (and thus applying the understanding). In this singular gesture, he warns us to be careful, while not heeding his own advice. As the reader of this text, it is impossible to land on one interpretation of the essay. The irony of the essay undermines the reader's ability to come to a definitive conclusion about the meaning of this, or any other, passage. Just as we think we have mastered this text, it slips through our fingers; it turns on itself and becomes its opposite, showing us that the desire for mastery was itself wrong-headed. Perhaps Schlegel does not mean this warning or maybe he does not mean it in the way we are reading it. Through repeated exposure to ironic texts, the reader practices her capacity to hold the two opposing and equally true interpretations of a passage like this one, and thus she arrives closer to the whole, which "contains" the unity of difference. In contrast with irony's indirect method for communicating a second meaning, an interpretation of the irony of this essay, which communicates directly, must first choose one meaning to express and then its opposite. That is, I tell you that the passage means "A" and then later, in the same account, I tell you that it means "not A" (just as Schlegel does on a smaller scale with his interpretation of fragment 216). Direct communication is limited, because I must select one interpretation to communicate first, and then another to express secondarily. However, in an indirect, ironic statement, the speaker or writer can utter one meaning directly while gesturing to a second, implied meaning. Thus, irony is a special linguistic technique that allows the one who dares to use it, to convey multiple, conflicting meanings.[68] At the meta-textual level, both interpretations of the text are equally plausible; that is, the text, as a whole, can be read as ironic or unironic. Clearly, if we interpret it as unironic, we limit its meaning; however, if we only read this text as ironic, we also limit its meaning insofar as we foreclose the possibility that it is not ironic. The realization of irony happens in a flash—in the experience of reading the text, there is a moment in which an additional meaning emerges; however, to hold onto this second meaning (i.e., that the text is ironic), merely reduces the text again to one meaning. If asked whether fragment 216 is ironic or whether the essay as a whole is ironic, the reader trained by the irony of Schlegel's essay would answer "yes and no." The yes and no are held together and not split apart; the text is ironic and it is not ironic.

"On Incomprehensibility" is a text that certainly produces something infinitely richer through pointing out its own limitations to its reader. However, I am not arguing that Schlegel is in complete control of the irony, as Eric Miller does; I will return to this theme of limitation and control in the following chapter to argue that Schlegel does not merely master the irony of the text, but rather that language is itself a limiting force on the author. Words, as Schlegel says in the essay, have relationships with each other, which is to say, meaning is not fully under our control as writers. Most writers (especially the analytic type) are motivated by the desire to remain in control of the resulting work and its effect on the audience; the ironic writer, by contrast, is comfortable with subjecting her work to the hazards inherent in writing itself. The ironic writer (and by extension, the ironic reader) has a different attunement to the text than the epistemological habits of control and mastery. These epistemological habits assume that rigidity and predictability are virtues and that the things, concepts, and ideas that are placed into rigid categories will stay put. The ironic writer, on the other hand, recognizes the limits of her control over the text and in light of that recognition, she cultivates agility, flexibility, and humility in relationship with it.

IRONY AND THE ROMANTIC IDEAL

As I said in the opening of this chapter, irony is integral to Schlegel's task, as a romantic philosopher, of approaching the Absolute. This task can be understood, in part, through the ideal of romantic poetry. Schlegel's most famous articulation of the ideal of romantic poetry is found in *Athenaeum* fragment 116:

> Romantic poetry is a progressive, universal poetry. Its aim isn't merely to reunite all the separate species of poetry and put poetry in touch with philosophy and rhetoric. It tries to and should mix and fuse poetry and prose, inspiration and criticism, the poetry of art and the poetry of nature; and make poetry lively and sociable, and life and society poetical; poeticize wit and fill and saturate the forms of art with every kind of good, solid matter for instruction, and animate them with the pulsations of humor.[69]

Schlegel goes on to say, in the same fragment, that romantic poetry "embraces everything purely poetic, from the greatest systems of art . . . to the sigh, the kiss that the poetizing child breathes forth in artless song." Schlegel does not limit romantic poetry to that which we normally call poetry (although he includes this too); rather, he allows poetry to encompass all creative activity [*poiesis*] including the sigh or the kiss of the "poeticizing child." Schlegel continues, "Romantic poetry is in the arts what wit is in philosophy, and what society and sociability, friendship and love are in life." That is, romantic poetry is that which enlivens, makes richer, and integrates; it is that which is inexhaustible, and as such, always incomplete.

Romantic poetry is not merely an aggregate of difference species of philosophy or the static unity of philosophy and poetry, but it is the aesthetic ideal that names the lively, animated, humorous, and playful bonding, separating, and joining that strives toward the Absolute. Wit is the tool used by the philosopher-poet-scientist, which facilitates the creation of chemical bonds in her experiments. As is now a famous proverb with its origins in *Hamlet*: Brevity is the soul of wit. Thus, it is not incidental that Schlegel wrote in fragments and short essays, but actually doing so makes his work wittier. Wit names the sudden meeting of ideas, which have long been separated.[70] Wit is connected to irony as both are forces that enable the association of seemingly disjointed or even contradictory ideas. Irony is a necessary tool for achieving a whole, which is lively and dynamic, rather than a mere static aggregate of parts.

The ideal of romantic poetry was crucial to the early romantic goal of *Bildung*, defined as the education of humanity or the development of all the characteristically human powers into an integral whole.[71] Frederick Beiser expresses it thusly in *The Romantic Imperative*: "To romanticize the world meant to make our lives into a novel or a poem, so that they would regain the meaning, mystery, and magic they had lost in the fragmented modern world."[72] The ideal of romantic poetry calls on us to turn our lives into a work of art, a poem, or an "endless novel."[73] The self-realized individual and the work of art are both organic wholes, which follow their own laws. Both exhibit freedom as the absence of external constraint and interference. In the organic model, every part belongs to the whole and is only comprehensible as a part of that whole; if everything is understood as part of a whole to which it belongs and gains its meaning, any interruption (as in the case of irony) would also be recuperated into the whole. Regarding irony, Beiser concludes: "If romantic irony is indeed directed against any claim to completion or closure, that is only because its aim is to goad our striving, to intensify our efforts, so that we approach closer to the ideal of a complete system."[74] By undercutting our attempts at a closed system, irony's role in that striving is to encourage us to continue to put the jigsaw puzzle together, rather than discouraging us in our attempts or showing us that they are entirely futile.[75] On this interpretation, the conflict between the Absolute and the relative, or the conditioned and the unconditioned, is irresolvable because our attempts to know the Absolute will limit it, demarcate it, and thus make the unconditioned into the conditioned. Likewise, complete communication is impossible, Beiser points out, because "any perspective is partial, any concept is limited, and any statement perfectible."[76] However, attempting complete communication is "*necessary* because we can approach the truth only if we strive to attain such an ideal." If we hold complete communication as an ideal toward which we are continually striving, we are able to achieve "a deeper perspective, a richer concept, a clearer statement of truth."[77] In order to protect Schlegel from the fate of being a proto-postmodern thinker, Frederick Beiser's interpretation focuses on the Absolute as an organic whole and the ideal of romantic poetry. Irony, on this holistic reading, is an interruption that encourages us in our task of striving toward the Absolute or the goal of turning our lives into an "endless novel."[78]

Although *Athenaeum* fragment 116 is the most frequently cited articulation of the ideal of romantic poetry, the activity of joining and fusing as a method for realizing the Absolute is reiterated in Schlegel's call for the unity of the disciplines, particularly philosophy and poetry. In the *Ideas* fragments, this imperative is articulated through the term "religion." In *The Literary Absolute*, Lacoue-Labarthe and Nancy draw attention to the "proper" meaning of "re-ligion" as the "possibility of linking together," rather than the particular religion of Christianity.[79] Moreover, many of the *Ideas* fragments take up the theme of the artist and employ religious references, such as the description of artists as Brahmins (the priestly caste in Hinduism), in order to convey the high calling of artistic life.[80] It is with this "proper" meaning of "re-ligion" as linking that Schlegel's *Ideas* fragments can be understood as a further articulation of and reflection on the ideal of romantic poetry. For example, in *Ideas* fragment 46, Schlegel writes, "Poetry and philosophy are, depending on one's point of view, different spheres, different forms, or simply the component parts of religion."[81] For when you try to combine poetry and philosophy, he claims, you end up with religion. In *Ideas* fragment 108, Schlegel instructs his readers that it is time to join philosophy and poetry, since whatever could be accomplished while they were separated has already been realized.[82]

Novalis also pursues this unity, especially in his *Romantic Encyclopedia*, where he attempts the task of joining philosophy and poetry with the natural sciences (mineralogy, biology) and social sciences (psychology, politics). The romantic vision of re-linking the disciplines, which have been separated through institutional and epistemological traditions, brings with it the prospect of transdisciplinary thinking through learning to be the ironic reader of irony. However, in combining disciplines we do not merely create a whole with fewer and fewer gaps. Rather, with the joining of two or more disciplines (as also with the meeting of two minds), the possibility of misunderstanding or incomprehension is amplified. As increasingly more disciplines are joined together, the opportunities for misunderstanding also increase, as well as the recognition, on the part of knowers, that there are more, rather than fewer, gaps in our understanding. In other words, as knowledge increases, so does the realization of what we do not know. In the Western philosophical tradition, thinkers have tended to focus on the spaces of presence, i.e., the aggregate or sum of information; but in focusing only on presence, we neglect the possibilities for misunderstanding that necessarily multiply as the work of building systems charges on.

CONCLUSION: ROMANTIC IRONY

Schlegel writes in *Ideas* fragment 74, "Join the extremes and you will find the true middle."[83] This fragment provides a guideline for how to think the romanticism of Schlegel's fragments along with their irony; in other words, Schlegel's project is romantic insofar as it continually searches for the Absolute—or as he puts it elsewhere, "Philosophy is the mutual search for omniscience."[84] But, at the same time, Schlegel's philosophy is thoroughly ironic. Dominant interpretations have either focused on Schlegel's romanticism or his account of irony. Frederick Beiser and Paul de Man represent exemplary models of each pole of interpretation. Beiser's reading focuses on the romanticism of Schlegel's philosophy through the ideal of romantic poetry, whereas de Man addresses Schlegel as a foremost thinker of irony. Irony, on Beiser's reading, merely encourages us in the philosophical activity of striving for the Absolute, whereas for de Man, irony undercuts all narratives and therefore also undercuts the striving to know the Absolute, an essential quality of romantic philosophy. One interpretation sees irony as an encouragement, the other as a mere discouragement or purely disruptive force. I join these two extremes, to place us in the "true middle," where Schlegel's position is to be found. If irony is disruptive (by turning the reader away from the literal meaning toward a figurative one, or by gesturing toward an additional meaning that stops us from closing the system), then this disruption is a necessary part of the striving for the whole, which I argued in the opening, must contain both presence and non-presence. Irony is not merely an encouragement separate from the striving itself, nor is it a disruption that makes this striving futile. Rather, it is a force, as the "form of paradox," that facilitates an encounter with absoluteness.

My argument is that irony does not merely "goad our striving" as Beiser contends, nor does it merely show us the impossibility of completing the system. Rather, it is literary technique *par excellence* that allows Schlegel to enact this striving toward the Absolute *with* his reader. I have emphasized the term *with* in the previous sentence, because, for Schlegel, the striving toward the Absolute happens in the sacred relationship of *symphilosophie*, which he is developing with the reader of his fragments. The conversation is the model for the communal striving toward the Absolute that we find in Schlegel's fragmentary project. This conversation not only happens between the author and her audience, but also occurs amongst the fragments and their multiple authors. Like the ideal of romantic poetry, the conversation is a dynamic, lively, and playful whole, which cannot exist without its component parts, i.e., its participants.

Irony is the technique that allows Schlegel to enact striving in communion with his reader. Because he cannot be physically present with her, Schlegel must use irony to tempt his reader to consider contradictory statements. Irony is the "form of paradox," which posits two claims that cannot be reconciled, without reducing one to the other or diluting either's meaning. In the ironic statement, both sides of the contradiction are present, as well as what is present in its absence: the openness of the ironic form that allows for both meanings to be held and further meanings to be generated. This space—the incomprehensibility or chaos that exceeds our systems—does not force the movement to take place, but rather makes it possible and ensures its continuation. Irony is the *form* that allows a paradox to be held (without mastering it); in this capacity, it not only achieves the metaphysically infinite, in its presentation of the whole, but also the mathematically infinite, by ensuring the unfolding of further meanings.

With Schlegel's transformation of the term, irony is no longer saying one thing and meaning another in such a way that the speaker conveys what she really means in a manner that would be predictable to her audience, e.g., through tone or context. Rather, the ironic statement intends two statements with opposing meanings. However, if the listener only takes one of these two meanings to be the case, i.e., she only partially understands the statement, then there is a failure of communication and, with it, no realization of absoluteness.

The encounter with absoluteness in the ironic fragments is an intuition of the whole that is tied to the performative function of irony within the text. That is, the experience of the Absolute can be traced back to particular textual moments, which is why I am calling this intuition of the whole "poetic mysticism." However, just because this intuition can be traced back to particular textual moments does not mean that any text can ever guarantee this experience for its reader; the text also depends on the reader in order to perform absoluteness. Additionally, the connection between the intuition of the whole and a text does not imply that a complete articulation of how irony facilitates that intuition can ever be provided, especially since it is irony that undercuts the completeness of all accounts.

In the following chapters, I continue to elaborate the difficulty that the writer attempting to communicate the Absolute faces, as well as how particular linguistic forms can disclose the Absolute without dominating or reifying it. As with the analysis of irony in this chapter, a central motif will be the subversion of a relationship to texts that aims at mastery. That is, texts that perform absoluteness do so by resisting their reader's attempts to grasp them, which means that all accounts of how they perform absoluteness will themselves be tentative and incomplete. After addressing Hegel's criticism of Schlegel (in chapter 2), I will analyze two poetic texts, which disclose the Absolute by receding away from meaning: the *Dao De Jing* chapter 3) and *Flow Chart* (chapter 4).

NOTES

1. "Kritische Fragmente von Friedrich Schlegel" in KFSA II, p. 153, CF 48. *"Ironie ist die Form die Paradoxen. Paradox ist alles, was zugleich gut und gro β ist."*
2. Schlegel, *Lucinde and the Fragments*, 148, CF 42.
3. Ibid., 155–156. KFSA II, p. 160, CF 108.
4. Eric Miller, "Masks of Negation: Greek *Eironeia* and Schlegel's Ironie," *ERR European Romantic Review* 8, no. 4 (1997), 361.
5. Ibid., 365.
6. Ernst Behler, *Irony and the Discourse of Modernity* (Seattle and London: University of Washington Press, 1990), 78.
7. Robert Solomon, *Morality and the Good Life: An Introduction to Ethics Through Classical Sources* (McGraw-Hill, 1984), 80.
8. In a recent, and quite literal, example of critique qua destruction, the artist Banksy's "Girl With Balloon" self-destructed after selling for $1.4 million at a Sotheby's auction. Because the work includes its own "destruction," it

communicates more than the straightforward version of "Girl With Balloon" could.

9. Miller, "Masks of Negation," 374–379.
10. Ibid.," 378.
11. Ibid.," 377.
12. Ibid.," 371. Similarly, Bärbel Frischmann argues that irony is productive insofar as it destroys the illusions that we have about knowledge and thereby moves us closer to a true understanding of the Absolute. In other words, irony is a skepticism about the truth, which, in its destructive capacity, only removes illusions of knowledge. Bärbel Frischmann, "Friedrich Schlegel's Transformation of Fichte's Transcendental into an Early Romantic Idealism," in *Fichte, German Idealism, and Early Romanticism*, ed. Daniel Breazeale and Tom Rockmore (Amsterdam: Rodopi, 2010), 353.
13. Miller, "Masks of Negation," 362.
14. "French Encyclopedia of 1765," quoted in Behler, *Irony and the Discourse of Modernity*, 76.
15. Recently, the rhetorical form of irony was clearly exhibited in Melissa McCarthy and Brian Tyree Henry's presentation of the Academy Award for costume design (February 2019). They told the audience that qualities of excellent costume design include "nuance and sophistication" and that excellent design does not distract from the film's plot. Meanwhile, their own costumes for the presentation were ostentatious and even included hand puppets. The irony of the presentation was communicated to the audience in a couple of predictable ways: the tone of the presenters and the context clues in the form of the costume each was wearing.
16. As one example of this form of argumentation, in *After Finitude*, Quentin Meillassoux uses the term "paradox" to denote the how correlationism's insistence against dogmatism actually leads it to fideism (as strong correlationism's *"other name"*). Quentin Meillassoux, *After Finitude: An Essay on the Necessity of Contingency* (London: Continuum Publishing, 2009), 48.
17. Paul de Man, *Aesthetic Ideology*, ed. Andrzej Warminski (Minneapolis: University of Minnesota Press, 1996), 164.
18. Ibid., 169.
19. Ibid., 166.
20. Ibid., 164–165.
21. Ibid., 164.
22. de Man, *Aesthetic Ideology*, 179. KFSA XVIII, p. 85.
23. Ibid; de Man translates "permanente Parekbase" as "permanent parabasis" rather than "permanent parekbasis." Etymologically, both terms have very similar meanings. "Parabasis" denotes a stepping to the side, and "parekbasis" denotes a stepping *out* to the side. "Parabasis" was the term that marked the

moments when the chorus directly addressed the audience in Old Attic Comedy, whereas "parekbasis" tended to be used by writers on rhetoric to note a digression in a text. In the sections where I am providing de Man's reading of Schlegel's fragment, I will retain the term as he translates it in his lectures. Because "parabasis" is the term that de Man actually uses, I will not alter the translation when I discuss his interpretation. Furthermore, since the meanings are so similar, I do not think this translation issue alters Paul de Man's reading of Schlegel. "Greek Word Study Tool," accessed March 25, 2016.

24. de Man, *Aesthetic Ideology*, 178.

25. Miller, "Masks of Negation," 366.

26. de Man, *Aesthetic Ideology*, 178.

27. Ibid.

28. Georgia Albert, "Understanding Irony: Three *essais* on Friedrich Schlegel," *MLN* 108, no. 5 (1993), 841–842.

29. de Man, *Aesthetic Ideology*, 179.

30. Schlegel, *Lucinde and the Fragments*, 155–156. KFSA II, p. 160, CF 108.

31. Hans Georg Gadamer, *Truth and Method*, trans. Joel Weinsheimer and Donald G. Marshall (New York: Seabury Press, 1975), 426.

32. Novalis, *Notes for a Romantic Encyclopedia: Das Allgemeine Brouillon*, ed. and trans. David W Wood (Albany: State University of New York Press, 2007), 108, entry 601.

33. Schlegel, *Lucinde and the Fragments*, 170. KFSA II, p. 176, AF 77.

34. Ibid., 189. KFSA II, p. 197, AF 206. I have amended the English translation to better reflect the German text. "*Ein Igel*," as it appears in the German, is more accurately translated as "hedgehog" than "porcupine" as it appears in Peter Firchow's *Friedrich Schlegel's Lucinde and the Fragments*.

35. Lacoue-Labarthe and Nancy, *The Literary Absolute*, 44.

36. Schlegel, *Lucinde and the Fragments*, 144, CF 14.

37. Ibid., 150, CF 65.

38. This analysis of the impossibility of arriving at the Absolute through an aggregate of parts is similar to Immanuel Kant's description of the mathematical sublime in the *Critique of the Power of Judgment*. There, Kant claims that the imagination's inadequacy—its inability to estimate a very large magnitude in nature—leads to the realization of a greater adequacy within ourselves, i.e., reason's idea of an absolute totality, which was the source for our desire to estimate the whole (through the imagination) in the first place. I am not claiming that Schlegel is repeating Kant's move here; the Absolute, for Schlegel, is not merely an idea of reason, which guides our pursuits, but which ultimately lies beyond the limits of human knowing.

39. Schlegel, *Lucinde and the Fragments*, 204. KFSA II, p. 215, AF 297.

40. A. W. Moore, *The Infinite* (Routledge, 1990), 1–2.
41. Ibid.
42. Schlegel, *Lucinde and the Fragments*, 167. KFSA II, p. 173, AF 53. "Es ist gleich tödlich für den Geist, ein System zu haben, und keins zu haben. Er wird sich also wohl entschließen müssen, beides zu verbinden."
43. Frederick C. Beiser, *German Idealism: The Struggle against Subjectivism, 1781–1801* (Cambridge, MA: Harvard University Press, 2002), 446.
44. Frederick C Beiser, *The Romantic Imperative: The Concept of Early German Romanticism* (Cambridge, MA: Harvard University Press, 2003), 126.
45. Schlegel, *Lucinde and the Fragments*, 145, CF 23.
46. Huch, Ricarda, *Die Romantik: Blütezeit, Ausbreitung und Verfall* (Tübingen: Wunderlich, 1951), quoted in Dennis McCort, "Jena Romanticism and Zen," *Discourse* 27, no. 1 (2005), 104.
47. In the lectures compiled in *Zen Mind, Beginner's Mind*, Shunryu Suzuki provides the example of a koan called "Polishing the Tile." In that koan, a student (Baso) is practicing in the meditation hall and is confronted by his teacher (Nangaku) who asks him what he is doing. He replies that he practicing zazen. The teacher asks "Why?" and he responds: "I want to attain enlightenment; I want to become a Buddha." The teacher then begins to polish a tile; when he is asked by the disciple why he is polishing a tile, he says that he is polishing the tile in order to make it a jewel. The student asks: "How is it possible to make a tile into a jewel?" The teacher replies: "How is it possible to become a Buddha by practicing zazen?" Just as a tile can never be polished into a jewel, Suzuki tells his students, practicing zazen can never make you into a Buddha; Buddhahood is only the ordinary mind; insofar as we think there is a goal of becoming a Buddha, we have created a division between ourselves and what we want to attain; we have created a gaining idea. Shunryu Suzuki, *Zen Mind, Beginner's Mind: Informal Talks on Zen Meditation and Practice* (New York: Weatherhill, Inc., 1970), 80–81.
48. "Über die Unverständlichkeit," in KFSA II, p. 366.
49. Ibid.
50. Ernst Behler, *Irony and the Discourse of Modernity*, 40.
51. "Über die Unverständlichkeit," in KFSA II, p. 366.
52. By filling in all the gaps for her reader's understanding, the analytic writer attempts to produce a text with a definite meaning. Most types of philosophical writing would fall into this category, as would advertising, insofar as both desire to produce a particular effect on their audience. An example, in the realm of art, where meaning is already exhausted or used up, is the case of kitsch.
53. The contemporary American comedian Bo Burnham utilizes a similar technique in his stand-up show "What." In an early bit, he demonstrates that

every statement he is making is ironic and therefore trains the audience in how to "read" the rest of the jokes.

54. Friedrich von Schlegel, "On Incomprehensibility (1800)," in *Classic and Romantic German Aesthetics*, ed. J. M. Bernstein (Cambridge, UK; New York: Cambridge University Press, 2003), 302. KFSA II, p. 368.

55. "Über die Unverständlichkeit," in KFSA II, p. 366.

56. Elaine Miller, "Romanticism and Continental Thought," presented during the Palgrave Workshop on German Romantic Philosophy, DePaul University, Chicago, IL, May 25, 2018.

57. Ernst Behler, *Irony and the Discourse of Modernity*, 78.

58. Schlegel, "On Incomprehensibility (1800)," 303–304.

59. Ibid., 304.

60. Schlegel, "On Incomprehensibility (1800)," 305. KFSA II, p. 370.

61. The language in this passage from "On Incomprehensibility" betrays Schlegel's anti-foundationalist project by pointing to what exceeds human knowing as a base for the structures humans create; in the third chapter, I will turn to the Daoist image of the wheel in order to put forth an alternate model for conceiving of the location of incomprehensibility or chaos.

62. Alison Stone, "Friedrich Schlegel, Romanticism, and the Re-enchantment of Nature," *Inquiry* 48, no. 1 (February 1, 2005), 7.

63. Schlegel, *Lucinde and the Fragments*, 155. KFSA II, p. 159, CF 104.

64. Daniel Breazeale elaborates this reading of a limit in terms of the Fichtean *Anstoß* in *Thinking Through the Wissenschaftslehre: Themes from Fichte's Early Philosophy* (New York: Oxford University Press, 2013).

65. "*Ideen*" in KFSA II, p. 263, I 71.

66. Schlegel, *Lucinde and the Fragments*, 246. KFSA II, p. 262, I 55.

67. Ibid., 247. KFSA II, p. 263, I 69.

68. Although I do not develop it here, it follows from this account that there is a difference in temporality for indirect communication, which does not adhere to the linear model described in the example of direct communication.

69. Schlegel, *Lucinde and the Fragments*, 175–176. KFSA II, pp. 182–183, AF 116.

70. Ibid., 166, AF 37.

71. Beiser, *Romantic Imperative*, 22.

72. Ibid., 19.

73. Ibid., 20.

74. Ibid., 34.

75. Beiser's reading fits nicely with Socrates' response to Meno's paradox in the *Meno*. That is, Socrates claims that the soul is immortal and that all learning is a recollection of what the soul already knows. Socrates admits that his response to Meno's paradox may be flawed; however, he claims that it is still

the better position because it encourages us in our pursuits, rather than leading us to believe that searching is futile, which would result in our becoming idle and fainthearted. Thus, Socrates' belief in the immortality of the soul operates like a regulative principle by encouraging our striving.

76. Beiser, *Romantic Imperative*, 129.
77. Ibid.
78. In contrast to de Man and Albert, Isaiah Berlin claims that the positing of contradictory statements leads to sincerity. In *The Roots of Romanticism*, he argues that early German romanticism was an attack on an Enlightenment view that saw the world as an enormous jigsaw puzzle. This Enlightenment view of the world held three primary assumptions, according to Berlin: All questions are answerable (if not by us, then by God), all the answers are knowable through the correct use of reason, and all these answers are compatible with each other. The only way to escape the "logical strait jacket" imposed by the laws of causality, the laws of the state, and aesthetic laws, according to the romantics on Berlin's reading, is to assert that for each statement or rule, there are three other contradictory but equally valid statements. This positing of at least three additional equally valid statements, leads, on Berlin's account, to one of the lasting effects of romanticism: sincerity. That is, even if we strongly disagree with someone, for the first time ever, we can respect that person for holding her view sincerely. Isaiah Berlin, *The Roots of Romanticism*, ed. Henry Hardy (Princeton, NJ: Princeton University Press, 1999), 21–23.
79. Lacoue-Labarthe and Nancy, *The Literary Absolute*, 78.
80. Schlegel, *Lucinde and the Fragments*, 255. KFSA II, p. 271, I 146.
81. Ibid., 245. KFSA II, pp. 260–261, I 46.
82. Ibid., 251. KFSA II, p. 267, I 108.
83. Ibid., 248. KFSA II, p. 263, I 74.
84. Ibid., 215. KFSA II, p. 216, AF 344.

2

TO BE IRONIC IS DIVINE: HEGEL'S AESTHETICS AND THE THREAT OF IRONY

By confronting the reader with the multiplication of meaning, irony introduces an opening into the text, the meaning of which is no longer fixed. Irony allows the text to say more; at the same time, it increases the potential for misunderstanding. Indeed, Schlegel was misunderstood by the readers of his ironic fragments and by his contemporary and sharpest critic: G. W. F. Hegel. In his *Lectures on Fine Art*, Hegel remarks that the Schlegel brothers (Friedrich and August Wilhelm) were "greedy for novelty," "non-philosophical," and unable to "claim a reputation for speculative thought."[1] He does not stop there, but goes on to attack irony as the "the most inartistic of all principles," to credit Friedrich Schlegel with the invention of the type of irony that he is criticizing, and to call Schlegel the divine ironic genius.[2] Clearly, as Charles Larmore puts it, Schlegel's irony "must have touched a nerve."[3] In Hegel's depiction of him, Schlegel is a divine ironic genius perched atop a high peak above the rest of the citizens; this ironic genius creates and destroys meaning at his whim and does not regard anything as independently solid or good. From this lofted standpoint, the "divine genius looks down . . . on all other men, for they are pronounced dull and limited, inasmuch as law, morals, etc., still count for them as fixed, essential and obligatory."[4] The divine ironic genius lives his life artistically by creating whatever he considers meaningful out of the pliable material of his own imagination.[5]

In this chapter, I will address Hegel's critique of Schlegelian irony. I begin with Hegel's critical remarks in order to situate Schlegel among one of his contemporaries and also to contextualize my own interpretation of Schlegel, which is, in part, a response to this critique. While I will address Hegel's pointed criticism of Schlegel, I will not do so to merely rescue Schlegel from an ungenerous interpretation of his work and, in the process, to treat Schlegel as a philosopher in his own right. Scholarship by many others has already accomplished this latter goal of placing Schlegel within the philosophical canon.[6] Rather than attempt to save Schlegel from Hegel's criticism of him, I will approach that criticism as an opportunity to bring certain elements of Schlegel's philosophy into sharper focus and, in particular, to examine why irony struck such a nerve with Hegel.

First, I will unpack why, for Hegel, the ironic viewpoint is dangerous and poses a threat to the objectivity of truth. A central feature of Hegel's criticism is the claim that the divine ironic genius' powers are left unchecked; this genius, whom Hegel calls divine, creates and destroys meaning at his own whim and only considers what he creates to be real. From this perspective, nothing is substantial or lofty enough to be left untouched. Then, I will argue that although Schlegel's fragments do indeed emphasize the two opposing poles of creation and destruction that distinguish the ironic genius' activity (as well as creative activity in general), these forces are met with an equal and thoroughgoing demand for restraint. A limit upon the writer or thinker's activity appears in the following forms in Schlegel's fragmentary writings: 1) As I proposed in the discussion of "On Incomprehensibility" in chapter 1, a limit is placed upon all attempts at system-building by what lies beyond the realm of human knowing; 2) the writer is limited by her desire to communicate to her audience; 3) the writer is limited by the fragmentary form itself; 4) the writer is limited by language, in particular by the relationships between words and their affinities with one another; 5) the writer is placed in check by irony as a force of restraint; and 6) the ironic philosopher is limited by her interlocuters.

HEGEL'S AESTHETICS AND THE THREAT OF IRONY

For Hegel, irony poses a double threat; it is dangerous in both its positive (creative) and negative (destructive) capacities. First, irony is a threat to the objectivity of truth insofar as the ego ("I" or "*Ich*") of the divine ironic genius is left unchecked. Second, irony, in its destructive capacity, is dangerously similar to comedy's role in Hegel's system of the fine arts and must be distinguished from the productive dissolution that comedy affords. I will first consider the danger of the unchecked ego (i.e., the positive, creative aspect) in the context of Hegel's discussion of beautiful art in his *Lectures on Fine Art*.[7] Then, I will examine comedy's role in the systematic progression of the fine arts and how its crucial transitional function is distinct from irony's destructive capacity for Hegel.

Hegel's criticism of the unchecked ego of the divine ironic genius is found within his appraisal of the role of beautiful art in reconciling free will with necessity. In his introductory remarks to the *Lectures*, Hegel describes the situation of the individual in modern culture as an "amphibious animal" [*Amphibie*].[8] As amphibious, human beings reside in two contradictory worlds. One world is the world of "abstract law," "the dead inherently empty concept," and "the spiritual in man" [*Geistige im Menschen*].[9] The other is a world characterized by the "abundance of individual phenomena," "the full concreteness of life," and "the flesh" [*Fleisch*].[10] As amphibious beings, humans are never fully at home; we are neither purely spirit, nor purely matter. The intellect has produced this division and now it is consciousness that is driven from one side to the other, from the "world of reality and earthly temporality" to the "realm of thought and freedom."[11] It is, according to Hegel, the very task of philosophy to "supersede the oppositions" by showing that neither possesses the truth, but rather "that truth lies only in the reconciliation and mediation of both, and that this mediation is no mere demand but what is absolutely accomplished and is ever self-accomplishing."[12] It is the vocation of art, beautiful or fine art in particular, "to unveil the *truth* in the form of sensuous artistic configuration."[13] Fine art occupies an elevated place in Hegel's system, because its task is the unveiling of Truth (albeit in a lesser, sensuous form).

It is within this context of the division between spirit and matter created by the intellect that Hegel charts the progression of the concept of the beautiful. In his *Lectures*, Hegel provides his audience with an historical account of the progression of the concept of the beautiful framed in terms of a peculiar Enlightenment problematic: how can a view of nature as mechanistic and rule-bound be reconciled with the free will requisite for morality? Hegel outlines the responses to this question provided by three thinkers: Immanuel Kant, Friedrich Schiller, and Johann Gottlieb Fichte. These thinkers are beginning to understand the beauty of art as being able to reconcile the activity of spirit, as characteristically free, with the passivity of nature as characteristically mechanistic and rule-bound. That is, there are certain beautiful objects that promote an experience that is different than our typical, appetitive engagement with the empirical world or with other selves; there are objects, in other words, that we encounter with disinterest, and that invite us into a relationship with them that is not merely ruled by self-interest, need, desire, or the logic of gratification.[14]

It is when Hegel turns to Fichte, in this section of the *Lectures* outlining the progression of the concept of the beautiful, that he launches into his critique of irony, in particular the ironic figure Schlegel whom he credits with the advent of divine irony.[15] Fichte's response to the Enlightenment problem that frames this discussion is unlike Kant's or Schiller's insofar as it does not point to the terms of establishing a harmony between freedom and necessity through the judgment or experience of the beautiful, but rather through the free act of a self-positing I as the "absolute principle of all knowing, reason, and cognition."[16]

Hegel outlines three points regarding what he will ultimately call the divine ironical genius, or the ironical standpoint as divine genius [*göttliche Genialität*], in connection with Fichte.[17] First, in Fichte's system, the absolute principle "of all knowing, reason and cognition" is the ego, which remains "abstract and formal" throughout.[18] Second, because the ego is an "abstract freedom and unity," it is simple, and every content is negated within it. Moreover, any content that would have value for the ego is created by it.[19] Nothing, Hegel argues, "is treated *in and for* itself and as valuable in itself, but only as produced by the subjectivity of the ego." When the ego is "lord and master of everything" [*Herr und Meister über alles*] then any meaningful content is posited by the ego, which means it can equally be destroyed by the same ego. Consequently, there is "no sphere of morals, laws, things human and divine, profane and sacred" that could not be dismantled by the ego.[20] For the ego, which creates and destroys all meaning, everything is a mere show [*Schein*]; nothing is independently real.[21]

The sense of the ego as "lord and master" is also conveyed through Hegel's repeated use of images of height. Jeffrey Reid observes that these images "conjure up references to solitude, vertigo, purity, and, most significantly with regard to objectivity, to distance from the ground."[22] Hegel's criticism picks up on an important feature of irony, which runs through all the definitions that I presented in chapter 1: distance. For both Greek *eironeia*, or dissimulation for personal gain, and the rhetorical definition, saying one thing but meaning another, distance is required. In both ironic utterances, there is a gap between the speaker's true position, on the one hand, and the position that she presents to her interlocuter, on the other hand. In Schlegel's transformation of irony, i.e., irony as the "form of paradox," distance becomes the space held by irony, which allows for two opposing meanings to be taken as true. This is a distance, as I said in chapter 1, which brings us closer.

By emphasizing the role of distance (without the elements of self-restraint that I will elaborate in this chapter), the ironist becomes, on Hegel's reading, the individual who is willing to put on any mask at will. Since none of the masks are her true position, it does not matter much which one she wears. Hegel compares this ironic stance to living one's life artistically; insofar as the ironist is the creator of everything that has meaning for her, she is equally capable of destroying those same creations. The ironic artist realizes—through her acts of self-creation and self-destruction—that nothing is stable, fixed, or binding; she looks down on people who do not yet realize, from their limited perspective, that the ego is the absolute principle of all knowing and that they too are the source of all meaning and knowledge for themselves. If the ego is the absolute principle for all knowing, then nothing is independently real. Truth is merely subjective and always relative to the ego as the "lord and master" who can freely create and destroy it. The ironic genius is divine because it is the source for everything that has meaning for it. The divine ironic genius' unchecked activity of creation and destruction poses a threat to the objectivity of truth; because the ironic genius is the source of all meaning, then a consequence of this position is that truth is merely subjective—always in relation to the ego that created it.

Thus far, irony's threat has been one of distance, which flattens out the world below. Next, I examine the proximity of irony and comedy in Hegel's *Lectures*. That is, irony, in its destructive capacity, is dangerously similar to Hegel's account of comedy, and therefore he must distinguish the productive moment of dissolution that comedy achieves from the threat of irony; whereas the former is a necessary moment in the system of the fine arts, the latter is dangerous to systematic philosophy. In order to understand this difference for Hegel, I will briefly sketch the progression of the beautiful or fine arts. Then, I will distinguish the destruction of comedy, as the "peak and dissolution" of art, from the destructive capacity of the ironic genius. Finally, I will contrast the exemplary figures for comedy and irony.

For Hegel, beautiful art unveils the truth through its harmonious reconciliation of universal and particular, content and form, or, put more concretely, the divine and its sensuous presentation. At each stage (symbolic, classical, romantic) in the development of beautiful art, the content of beautiful art is a particular, historically situated conception of the divine and the form is the material, internal or external, that is molded in order to sensuously manifest the divine. For example, sculpture is the sensuous form given to the ancient Greek gods. The Ideal for beautiful art is the unity of content and form, or the divine and its sensuous manifestation: symbolic art is the striving for this Ideal, classical art is its attainment, and romantic art is the transcendence of this Ideal. The system of the fine arts begins with architecture and unfolds toward its Ideal through sculpture, painting, music and poetry. In its attempt to attain the Ideal for art, the unity of meaning and shape, art transcends the shape (the materiality) of art. Art transcends precisely what makes it the artistic manifestation of truth, and moves into what Hegel calls the "prose of thought [*Prosa des Denkens*]."[23] Through its self-transcendence, art becomes "for us" moderns "a thing of the past."[24] Art no longer holds the highest vocation of manifesting the divine; art's role has been superseded by philosophy. The transition from the attainment of the Ideal in classical art to the transcendence of it in romantic art occurs in the classical form of art with comedy, a subcategory of dramatic poetry.

Comedy, specifically ancient Greek comedy, achieves the "peak" [*Gipfel*] and the "dissolution" [*Auflösung*] of art "altogether" [*überhaupt*].[25] The dissolution of art is complete with comedy insofar as comedy cancels out both the form and content proper to art. As a subspecies of poetry, comedy annuls art's form, or its materiality. Like music, poetry retains the material of sound, but, unlike music, it only retains sound as a sign of an idea.[26] Comedy not only dissolves the materiality proper to art's form, but it also dissolves art's proper content (i.e., the divine). Comedy cancels out art's proper content because the issues encountered by the comic individuals, and their eventual resolution in the action of the play, remain at the level of the human. This shift in content—from the divine to the human—occurs in the transition from ancient Greek tragedy to comedy. In tragedy, the heroic individuals embody, like sculptures, particular ethical and religious powers. In the specific example of *Antigone*, the ethical and religious powers of the family and the gods of the underworld are embodied by Antigone, whereas Creon embodies the powers of the state and the god Zeus. A contradiction arises between two conflicting sets of ethical demands, those of the gods of the family and those of the gods of the state, and this conflict comes to the fore through two individual wills.[27] Due to their "tragic firmness of will," both heroic individuals are led to their eventual demise.[28]

In comedy, the gods of the *polis* no longer determine right and wrong or reward and punishment, but rather these matters are left up to the very human comic individuals.[29] Comic actors are ordinary people, not nobility, who use colloquial speech and rely heavily on toilet humor and obscenities. Comic action is not concerned with the tragic conflict between two heroic individuals, but rather broader affairs of the city, such as the governance of the *polis*. In comedy, Hegel says, it is "the general public interests that are emphasized, statesmen and their way of steering the state, war and peace, the people and its moral situation, philosophy and its corruption and so forth."[30]

Hegel's exemplar of the comic-poet is Aristophanes, whom he calls a "true patriot" and "the best of citizens," because he shows the Athenians the contradiction between the true essence of political life and the subjective attitudes held by Athenians who should give actuality to this essence.[31] Stephen C. Law explains, "True comedy never attacks virtue" but rather "vice masquerading in the pretense of virtue." Law continues, "Aristophanes' goal, as Hegel sees it, is to point out the hypocrisy in Athenian society: the Athenians have correctly ascertained the true and substantive, but they refuse to take their own values seriously, and, so, have spiraled into a suicidal *reductio ad absurdum*."[32] In Aristophanes' *Assemblywomen*, the male citizens of the *polis* are poorly managing the affairs of the city and the women decide to take over governance. Aristophanes presents the shortcomings of Athenian democracy in terms of the contradiction between the essence of democracy and the subjective attitudes of citizens.

What is of primary interest for Hegel in the comedies of Aristophanes is how his plays are comedic at the systematic level. That is, comedy presents a contradiction between the ideal and the real and what we find so humorous, what makes us laugh, is the sharp contrast between the two sides of this contradiction. On one side of the contradiction lies the ideal of democracy or more precisely its actuality, i.e., the full correspondence of the idea of democracy with its realization. On the other side of the contradiction, we find the subjective attitudes of the citizens of the *polis*—the men who do not take governance seriously. Comic action exaggerates its subject matter, and, by exaggerating, it can more distinctly convey the truth of the contradiction that is already found, albeit in a subtler form, in society. The contradiction, and its eventual resolution when the women successfully take over running the *polis*, is portrayed through the dramatic action and dialogue of the play. Although a resolution is achieved in comedy, the audience is alerted to the absurdity of this resolution in a couple of ways. First, the women are only able to take over governing the *polis* through their cunning and ability to deceive, and not through honest methods. Second, the play ends with a scene in which an older woman is chasing around a young and attractive man in order to enforce a new policy that requires him to first copulate with her if he wishes to have intercourse with a young and beautiful woman. The play does not end with a reasoned analysis of the virtues of communal living, but rather with an extreme, and quite absurd, portrayal of the enactment of that communal law. In Law's terms, this is the "suicidal *reductio ad absurdum*." The play takes the idea that the *polis* ought to be organized like the home to its absurd conclusion.

Hegel is careful to distinguish the dissolution that comedy affords, of an already null or contradictory phenomenon, "an oddity," or "a *supposedly* tenable principle and firm maxim" from the dissolution produced by divine ironic genius.[33] Significantly, for Hegel, the content negated in comedy is an already null or contradictory phenomenon, e.g., the gap between the ideal of democracy and its instantiation in ancient Athens. The ironic genius, on the other hand, does not merely destroy that which is null or contradictory, but rather—because she only considers what she creates to be real (or considers everything that exists to be her creation)—there are no limits on what she is willing to destroy. Irony is divine and perched above the realm of the human, whereas the comedian (in particular the exemplar Aristophanes) is "the best of citizens" who presents the truth through the issues and vernacular of ordinary people.[34] If the purpose of art is to sensuously manifest the Divine, then the ironical Divine also poses a threat to this ultimate aim of art. That is, if the Divine is ironical, then it remains separate from, or perched above, the realm of the human. With the ironic work of "art," it is not the case that the Divine disappears from the work of art (through art's own progression), but rather that the Divine never becomes manifest in the first place, which perhaps explains why Hegel calls irony the most inartistic principle.

If Aristophanes is the "best of citizens" then Schlegel—or the divine ironic genius—is among the worst. Because of his distance from the ground, or the ordinary people, the ironic genius is a threat in both his creative and destructive powers, since, in either capacity, he does not respect anything outside of his own creation. If everything that has meaning for him is his creation, then truth only has subjective value. Moreover, if everything that exists is his own creation, then it can equally be destroyed by him. There is nothing objectively real, which is not subject to his destructive power. From his lofted position, he may feel pity for the other citizens, because they do not realize that the laws and morals that they regard as binding are merely the result of the creative powers of the imagination.[35]

In the following sections, I respond to Hegel's sharp criticism of Schlegel as the divine ironic genius whose creative and destructive capacities are left unchecked and thus a danger to the objectivity of truth. I will argue that Schlegel is not the solitary ironic genius who regards truth as merely his own subjective creation. To show this, I will highlight several modes of relationality that place constraints upon the ego in Schlegel's philosophical project. The emphasis on relationality and restraint in Schlegel's fragments not only illustrates that he is indeed not the absolute ego, but also, these moments support the claim that restraint is necessary in the communication of the Absolute. That is, paradoxically, it is restraint (and not unlimited creative power) that is needed in order to realize the Absolute.

THE DESIRE TO COMMUNICATE

In his Critical fragments, Schlegel focuses on restraint in terms of the self-restraint needed in order to write well. He explains, in Critical fragment 37, that in order to write well on a subject, the writer "shouldn't be interested in it any longer." If the author is still in "the process of discovery and inspiration," she will want to "blurt out everything" that she knows and she "fails to recognize the value and dignity of self-restriction"; if an individual isn't able to restrict herself then she will be restricted by the world; she will be a slave to the world.[36] In order to restrain herself, the writer must have distance from her topic. Without the capacity for self-restraint, one merely acts on impulse; it is restraint, which allows for an opening in which a choice is possible. A lack of self-restraint is an error when encountered with "young geniuses" but it is "a legitimate prejudice of old bunglers."[37] A writer, Schlegel continues, who is incapable of keeping anything to herself is to be pitied. This standard of self-restraint not only applies to writing, but also to conversations, which, if friendly, can be broken off at any point. At the end of this rather lengthy fragment about restraint (perhaps an ironic twist), Schlegel warns against exaggerating self-restriction.[38] Like the "irony of irony" in "On Incomprehensibility," there is a "restraint of restraint" operating here; the one who practices self-restraint must have restraint in the practice of it. Without restraint, even a friendly conversation cannot be cut off and the writer cannot write well because she merely blurts out everything she knows. However, creation is also necessary in order for the writer to invent or to give herself over to inspiration. An exaggeration of self-restriction would inhibit the work from being produced at all, but an absence of self-restriction altogether would make for a poorly written work, i.e., a work that did not successfully communicate ideas. Like the necessity of the mind [*Geist*] to both have and not have a system as expressed in *Athenaeum* fragment 53, the good writer must balance the forces of creation, inspiration, and inventiveness *as well as* restraint, critique, and destruction.[39]

Elaborating his concern about writing well, Schlegel claims in Critical fragment 33 that "[the] overriding disposition of every writer is almost always to lean in one of two directions: either not to say a number of things that absolutely need saying, or else to say a great many things that absolutely ought to be left unsaid. The former is the original sin of synthetic, the latter of analytic minds."[40] The sin of the analytic writer is to fill in all the gaps, leaving no latitude for the reader's interpretation. In contrast, the synthetic writer sins insofar as she depends too much on her reader to create the meaning of the text with her, e.g., by filling in the gaps or by deciphering the necessity of the empty spaces that the author has left in the text. Most writers do not find the middle ground that Schlegel is attempting to describe, but rather lean either toward saying too much or saying too little. As a synthetic writer himself, Schlegel is most likely to commit the sin of saying too little; however, if the objective is the intuition of the Absolute, then this sin appears to be the less grave one, insofar as leaving room in the text brings its reader closer to the whole.

Schlegel's fragments repeatedly demand that the good writer, the one who wishes to communicate rather than merely express herself, must practice self-restraint. The audience is the impetus to write at all and the check placed upon the writer if she wishes to communicate ideas effectively and not merely bombard her reader with a mass of undigested information. In order to communicate, the writer must use restraint to balance the forces of self-creation and self-destruction. The practice of self-restraint in the writing process requires distance from the subject matter. However, distance is not operating in the same way as it does in Hegel's depiction of the ironic genius, whose elevated standpoint allows her to create and destroy meaning at whim and who looks down on those who have not yet reached the loftiness of her divine standpoint. Rather, distance is a requirement for the writer who wishes to communicate well, i.e., to find a way to express herself to her audience without either saying too much or too little. Being too close to the subject matter is dangerous, because if the writer is still absorbed in it, she will want to express everything she has discovered. Being too far from the subject is equally problematic, because then she does not say enough to convey her ideas to her audience. Distance, in other words, does not lead to unlimited creation and destruction, but rather to the balance of creation and destruction needed in order to write well.

RESTRAINT IN STYLE: FRAGMENTS

By writing in short, self-contained fragments, Schlegel demonstrates the very self-restraint that he calls for from the good writer and thinker. Moreover, Schlegel does not merely write in fragments out of laziness, irresponsibility, or a lack of philosophical rigor; his fragmentary style is not arbitrary, but rather the formal counterpart to romantic philosophy. As I sketched in the introduction, the philosophical viewpoint of the early German romantics can be distinguished from their predecessors in several key ways: 1) it is anti-foundationalist (i.e., it views the search for foundations as an infinite regress); 2) it begins in the midst of things; 3) it does not aim at closure, but rather views philosophizing as an infinite, communal activity; and 4) it emphasizes wit as a means for the playful fusing of ideas. These key features of romantic philosophy are reflected in the fragmentary form that philosophy takes. There is no fragment that provides a first principle or foundation for the system of fragments, nor is there any fragment that provides an ultimate conclusion. There is no particular order in which the fragments must be read or a definitive organization of the fragments that would yield a completed system. Each fragment is simultaneously an individual that can be approached on its own and part of a larger collection, a conversation amongst the hundreds of fragments and their multiple authors. As Novalis puts it in his Logological fragments: "Everything is seed."[41]

Although the fragments can be read in any order, how we read them, the chain or garland we string them into, will alter their meanings, at least in part. If I string together one garland of fragments, you get one sense of Schlegel's project, whereas a different garland gives a different sense. This is another issue with Paul de Man's reading, which I presented in chapter 1. He overdetermines the meaning of Schlegelian irony by focusing on only one fragment from an unpublished collection. Although the meaning of an isolated, individual fragment can be completely coherent, it can overdetermine the interpretation of Schlegel's philosophy. Each presentation of the fragments will bring aspects of Schlegel's philosophy into sharper relief—certain meanings will come to the fore or fade into the background. However, there is no organization that is conclusive; as intentionally fragmentary, the project is always open, never complete; the fragments are open to new interpretations like "[a] classical text," which "must never be entirely comprehensible."[42]

It is not only the reader who impacts the meaning of the fragments through the order she chooses to read them, the fragments also train the reader's mind. Because the fragments invite their reader to tarry with contradictory claims, they cannot be merely comprehended (that is, contained by the reader's understanding). And, insofar as they cannot be merely comprehended, they train the reader to have an agile mind and thereby bring her nearer to the Absolute, which must, like the fragment, contain presence, non-presence, and the space (or form) that allows for their co-emergence. As I argued in chapter 1, irony is the *form* that facilitates the holding of opposites. If irony entails distance (via the creation of space), it is a distance that brings us closer. Distance is emphasized in the gaps between the fragments—the empty space on the page between each numbered fragment—that exhorts the reader to pause before moving on to the next one. This format encourages the reader to sense the separateness of each of the fragments and to slow down before moving on too quickly to the following fragment. This space between fragments resists the reader's attempts to merely consume and digest the meaning of each fragment, and it dissuades her from too hastily proceeding to connect one fragment's meaning seamlessly with another's. At the same time, this space draws the reader into the text; it invites her to interpret it and elaborate its meaning.

The fragments are not only in dialogue with the reader, but also in a conversation amongst themselves. They are comprised of many voices both literally and figuratively. The fragments are literally polyphonous in terms of the multiple authors of the fragments (the Schlegel brothers, Schleiermacher, Novalis), but they also figuratively contain a multiplicity of voices in what Michel Chaouli terms the "endless chatter" that takes place among them; this chatter is not incidental, since the fragments have the "structure of conversation" embedded in their very form.[43] The fragments never appear alone; they always appear in the plural and point to each other.[44] Each fragment points beyond itself, to another fragment, elsewhere. The fragments are the site where the striving of romantic philosophy takes place; they are the laboratories for philosophy as experimentation. I will focus on this latter aspect of the fragmentary form in the following section.

THE ROMANTIC EXPERIMENT: FRAGMENT LABORATORIES

In the opening to "On Incomprehensibility," Schlegel proclaims that "words often understand themselves better than those who use them" and that words belong to a "secret brotherhood."[45] Taking this claim seriously (and literally), Michel Chaouli argues that chemistry can serve as a model for Schlegel's fragmentary project because "[it] looks for affinities and attractions between disjointed elements without lending them final coherence."[46] In the same way that some elements appear to be drawn to one another much more than others, at the level of language, certain letters, morphemes, phrases, or words attract one another; they have affinities for one another, while others do not. Adopting chemistry as the conceptual model or allegory for poetics allows for a theory of poetry (or language) to emerge in which the poem is not merely the result of the genius who intentionally created or produced it (as in the model of the artist as sovereign). Instead, on this chemical model, there is an on-going and unending process of "combinatorial formation and deformation" of which the poet is not in full control.[47] The genius, on this model, is the one who risks exposing her writing forces beyond her control.

If we unpack this allegory of chemistry, the elements are the letters, morphemes, and words in question, and the laboratory is the fragment itself. The fragment is the site where the experiments of dividing and mixing take place.[48] There are several consequences of this chemical model for interpreting Schlegel's fragmentary writings. First, the "number and range of possible linguistic expressions [increases] dramatically."[49] On the chemical model, the combination of elements, which is not entirely under the control of the writer, may produce entirely novel or meaningless combinations. This growth in the number of possible linguistic expressions leads to a second consequence of this model: Each utterance has "something human as well as something nonhuman about it."[50] On the one hand, an utterance would not exist without human beings and their motivations for writing or speaking (although these motives are not always fully conscious). At the same time, however, each utterance "partakes of a combinatorial system anteceding us, external to us, and accessible to others," and thus each utterance must submit to "an apparatus beyond the reach of any single human."[51]

Third, the chemical model highlights the autonomy of art. Art is not only liberated from social pressures about what art ought to do or accomplish, but even from the artist; art becomes *"automatic."*[52] Incomprehensibility becomes the index for the autonomy of art; the more autonomous art is, the more it can tolerate or promote incomprehensible statements.[53] Fourth, the written fragments become the laboratories in which these experiments transpire; insofar as the chemical model underscores the role of experimentation and experiments require a degree of control, art works must be written down and isolated.[54]

This chemical model for poetry introduces an additional layer of restraint into Schlegel's fragments. On this model, the author is no longer the master in complete control of her work, but rather an individual who is willing to take the risks inherent in writing—to expose herself and her work to forces larger than herself. The fragments are not merely the result of a sovereign ironic artist wielding the power to create and destroy; rather, they are the location for experimentation to take place; they are the site where the joining and mixing happen and where words and sounds find affinities with one another. Restraint is no longer merely self-restraint; rather, restraint also refers to the limits placed upon the writer by language itself, i.e., the ways language exceeds any one writer's control. Or, as Judith Norman puts it, philosophy, by virtue of its linguistic structure, always incorporates an element of incomprehensibility, and thus even the cleverest philosopher can be "outwitted by language."[55] Additionally, the publication of the *Athenaeum*, as the joint endeavor of the romantic circle, undermines the notion of the genius as a solitary individual and further augments the likelihood of novel combinations and meanings through the plurality of voices represented within it. I return to this definition of genius that emerges out of the chemical model in the final chapter on John Ashbery, where I discuss the techniques by which Ashbery introduces contingency and chance into his poems.

IRONY AS (SELF-)RESTRAINT

Schlegel communicates the connection between a familiarity with irony and an intimacy with the limits of communication in his description of Socratic irony in Critical fragment 108. Insofar as irony undercuts our attempts to communicate completely, it is the ironist who regularly feels the tension "between the impossibility and the necessity of complete communication."[56] However, as I have been arguing, by limiting our attempts—by showing us there is another meaning and that we do not have the last word—irony actually brings us in contact with absoluteness. Irony operates ironically: It limits us and in so doing reveals more than we could know without it. It discloses by limiting.

Although Schlegel cites Socrates as the exemplar of irony in this fragment, he is simultaneously transforming the meaning of irony from its ancient Greek sense as well as its traditional, rhetorical meaning, as I argued in chapter 1. In the ancient Greek sense, the ironist dissimulates, or wears a mask, in order to accomplish some ulterior motive. I sketched Eric Miller's interpretation of Schlegel's resuscitation of the term; for Miller, the *eiron* is the one who dissimulates, but in order to achieve a higher-order aim; in this case, irony facilitates self-restraint through the self-critical work, but this limitation (qua critique) is merely the appearance of limitation. Restraint was only the appearance of restraint, which was under the control of the artist all along.[57]

My argument, to the contrary, is that, with Schlegelian irony, restraint is no longer purely self-restraint; the artist is no longer the sovereign who has complete mastery over the material and who only seems to encounter a limitation to her work. Rather, irony actually functions as a restraint in two ways. First, irony limits each of the terms in the fragment by holding them in tension with each other; in the ironic fragment, neither term is permitted to define the meaning of the fragment on its own. Irony is able to hold two contradictory statements together in a way that does not diffuse or dissolve either of the statements, and thus it thwarts its interlocutor's attempts to merely choose one side or the other of an opposition. This first form of restraint is included in Miller's account as irony's ability to balance self-creation and self-destruction. But, there is a second form of restraint that is produced by the first: Irony's doubling of meanings creates an opening in the text that allows for the possibility of additional meanings (which is to say previously unconsidered meanings) to emerge. Irony shows the one who writes or thinks ironically that the realm of human understanding is limited by that which exceeds it. The ironic "genius" is precisely the one who is best acquainted with the limitation that irony poses to our attempts at system-making. As Schlegel says of Socrates, he understood both the necessity for complete communication and the impossibility of it, because it is precisely irony that shows us that no final word is possible. Through irony, we realize that all our attempts at knowing are exceeded by that which we do not know or cannot know.

THE MUTUAL SEARCH

Finally, in Schlegel's writings, there is an emphasis, contrary to the picture of the solitary divine ironic genius, on the communal effort of philosophizing. Schlegel is engaged in a project of *symphilosophie* as the "mutual search for omniscience."[58] For the romantics, the activity of philosophizing is not a solitary pursuit; but rather, it is a communal endeavor; it is an activity we engage in together, in conversation with one another. Referring to a line in Lessing's "Nathan the Wise," Schlegel succinctly captures his relationship to philosophy, to the divine, and to the Absolute—the pursuit of which is a communal effort that belongs to no one person: "At the words 'his philosophy, my philosophy,' one is always reminded of that line in *Nathan*: 'Who owns God? What kind of God is that who belongs to a man?'"[59]

The emphasis on *symphilosophie* is encountered on several levels in Schlegel's philosophical writings. The *Athenaeum* journal was not the pinnacle achievement of a singular philosophical genius; instead, in it, the reader discovers the communal project of a group and the mixture of the voices of its contributing authors. This communal project is mirrored in the fragments; they are individuals, and yet, like the members of the romantic circle, they are always in conversation with each other; the fragments refer to each other; each fragment is an isolated whole, and yet always in dialogue with other fragments. *Symphilosophie* extends beyond the authors of the fragments and the relationship amongst the fragments themselves to the relationship between the writer and her audience. The synthetic writer who practices *symphilosophie* is not simply delivering a monologue, but rather she is entering into a dialogue with other thinkers and with her audience; the ironic fragments depend on their reader, whom they also simultaneously train to understand them.

Symphilosophie is also expressed in terms of a philosophical friendship, both with our peers and in the inner relationship with ourselves.

In a fragment included in Novalis' *Blütenstaub* fragments, Schlegel writes, "[if] in communicating a thought, one fluctuates between absolute comprehension and absolute incomprehension, then this process might already be termed a philosophical friendship. For it's no different with ourselves. Is the life of a thinking human being anything else than a continuous inner symphilosophy?"[60] Here, Schlegel presents *symphilosophie* as an inner dialogue or conversation, a movement within oneself between comprehension and incomprehension. An inner dialogue is not merely the overcoming of incomprehension in order to know; *symphilosophie* is not accomplished through the removal of anything alien that would lead to misunderstanding. Rather, incomprehensibility is part of the philosophical friendship we have with ourselves and with others. Schlegel describes his philosophical friendship with Novalis, who died in 1801 at the age of twenty-eight, by saying that what he now thinks, Novalis had already thought, and that between the two of them "[there] are misunderstandings that only serve to confirm the greatest shared understanding."[61]

CONCLUSION

> What am I proud of, and what can I be proud of as an artist? Of the decision that separated and isolated me forever from everything ordinary; of the work that divinely surpasses every intention, and whose intention no one will ever probe entirely; of the ability to worship the perfection I have encountered; of the awareness that I can stimulate my fellows to do their best, and that everything they create is my gain.[62]

In this, *Ideas* fragment 136, Schlegel conveys the multiple ways that, as an artist, he is limited by what exceeds him: his audience, his peers, and those aspects of the work that are not completely under his control. In this chapter, I have focused on the notion of limitation or restraint as it appears in various forms in Schlegel's fragmentary project in order to respond to Hegel's characterization of Schlegel as the divine ironic genius; the ironic genius is divine insofar as he is perched above the rest of humanity and lives his life artistically by creating and destroying anything that has meaning for himself at his own whim. For Hegel, this divine ironic genius presents a threat to systematic philosophy in two ways: 1) if meaning is only the result of the creative power of the ironic genius' imagination, then nothing is objectively true and all content that is created by the ironic genius can equally be destroyed by him; 2) irony, in its destructive capacity, is dangerously similar to the productive dissolution that comedy accomplishes in the system of fine art, and therefore must be distinguished from it. My aim has been to respond to this critique by highlighting the role of restraint and relationality in Schlegel. My claim is that Schlegel is not the absolute ego capable of producing only subjective truths, but rather that irony plays a central role in the earnest, communal endeavor toward the Absolute.

First, as I argued in chapter 1, in the short essay "On Incomprehensibility," which was aimed at the readers who misunderstood his fragments, Schlegel warns the philosophers of his time against attempting to make everything fully comprehensible through the application of the thin, watered-down type of rationality, i.e., the understanding in its dismembering capacity. The understanding disenchants nature by analyzing it; it attempts to encompass the universe within the bounds of the structures of human knowing, and, in the process, reduces and destroys its meaning. Given the understanding's propensity to break apart, destroy, and disenchant through the same methods by which it attempts to analyze and comprehend, Schlegel asks his readers whether incomprehensibility is really something so contemptible and urges them to practice restraint in their attempts to comprehend everything. Schlegel distinguishes the thin, watered-down type of reason (the sub-species referred to as the understanding) from reason that is thick and fiery and which makes wit witty. This latter species of reason does not break apart what it seeks to know, but rather it facilitates the process of chemical bonding necessary for realizing the Absolute. Furthermore, Schlegel argues that truly possessing a multifaceted and universal view is not accomplished through creating an ever-expansive system using the understanding, but instead by cultivating a sense for that which lies outside our attempts at system-making and operates as both an impetus for the production of meaning and a check or limit on what the understanding can grasp.

Second, I turned to Schlegel's fragments concerning the art of writing well. In these fragments, Schlegel argues that in order to communicate, rather than to merely express oneself, the writer must have a concern for her audience. An audience is an impetus to write at all, and also a limit or check on her attempts if her aim is the communication of ideas. The writer who communicates well practices self-restraint of creation, destruction, and restraint itself. Restraint requires distance from the subject matter and ensures that the writer is neither possessed by the subject matter, nor forgetful of it.

Third, in its form, the fragment is the counterpart to the imperative to practice self-restraint, which the writer must obey if she wishes to communicate to her audience and not merely express herself. The fragment is one of the favored modes for the communal activity of philosophizing, which emphasizes anti-foundationalism, beginning in the middle, non-closure, and the brevity required for wit. Fourth, the writer is limited by language, in particular by the relationships that words have with each other. In an experimental conception of writing, the fragments are the laboratories and the elements are the words and word parts, some of which have greater affinities to each other than others. The writer, on this model, is the one who is willing to take a risk, to subject herself to the risks inherent in writing itself, and to the possibility of incomprehensibility that arises, in part, because the entire edifice of language far exceeds any one writer and is thus always, in some ways, out of her control.

Fifth, irony accomplishes restraint by holding contradictory ideas in tension within the fragment and, in so doing, it shows its reader that her attempts at knowing are always incomplete. Finally, for the romantics, the activity of philosophizing is a communal effort. This community includes thinkers spanning space and time, the chatter of the fragments, as well as the role of philosophical friendship.

Hegel's critique picks up on a central aspect of the traditional meanings of irony before Schlegel's transformation of the term: distance. Distance from the ground and from her peers emboldens the ironist to put on and take off any mask at will. We could simply dismiss Hegel's characterization of Schlegel as inaccurate; however, his critique raises a legitimate worry about irony in general and provides the opportunity to distinguish Schlegelian irony from its predecessors. The requisite distance for the other forms of irony to perform their functions does indeed make irony a threat to truth. However, for Schlegelian irony, distance is conceived of as the space that is necessary in order to bring irony's interlocutor closer to the Absolute. The ironic statement includes the space necessary to hold two contradictory statements without allowing their conflation; in its form, the ironic fragment expresses absoluteness. I will elaborate the role of space or emptiness in the next chapter, where distance will re-emerge as the emptiness at the heart of the images used to describe the *Dao* in the *Dao De Jing*. The *Dao De Jing* offers resources, particularly in its use of paradox and metaphor, for expressing a dynamic and generative Absolute, without at the same time reifying or mastering what it seeks to describe.

NOTES

1. Georg Wilhelm Friedrich Hegel, *Aesthetics: Lectures on Fine Art*, trans. T. M. Knox, 2 vols. (Oxford: Clarendon Press, 1975), 63. G. W. F. Hegel, *Vorlesungen über die Ästhetik*, ed. Eva Moldenhauer and Karl Markuss Michel, 3 vols. (Frankfurt am Main: Suhrkamp, 1970), 3: 572. Hereafter cited as VA. (These three volumes also comprise vols. 13, 14, and 15 of the *Werke in zwanzig Bänden*.)

2. Ibid., 68.

3. Charles E. Larmore, *The Romantic Legacy* (New York: Columbia University Press, 1996), 80.

4. Hegel, *Aesthetics: Lectures on Fine Art*, 66. VA, 3: 572.

5. There are certainly places in Schlegel's fragments where one can find support for the claim that the ironic genius is perched above the rest of society, at a great height. For example, in *Athenaeum* fragment 264, he writes, "You shouldn't try to symphilosophize with everyone, but only with those who are *à la hauteur.*" In *Athenaeum* fragment 168, Schlegel asks what type of philosophy is left for the poet and responds that it is a "creative philosophy that originates in freedom and belief in freedom, and shows how the human spirit impresses its law on all things and how the world is its work of art." And, in *Ideas* fragment 146, Schlegel says of artists: "Even in their outward behavior, the lives of artists should differ completely from the lives of other men. They are Brahmins, a higher caste: ennobled not by birth, but by free self-consecration." Although these examples seem to support Hegel's claims about the ironic genius, my argument throughout this book is that irony is not a mere technique to achieve distance, but rather the very means by which contact with the Absolute is achieved. I will return to some of these claims in the final chapter when I discuss the "sacred relationship" of *symphilosophie*. Schlegel, *Friedrich Schlegel's Lucinde and the Fragments*, 200, 183, 255. KFSA II, pp. 210, 191–192, 271, AF 264, AF 168, I 146.

6. In particular, I am deeply indebted to the work of Elizabeth Millán Brusslan, Frederick Beiser, Dalia Nassar, Manfred Frank, and Ernst Behler.

7. Hegel gave his lectures on aesthetics in 1818 in Heidelberg and in Berlin during the winter semester of 1820/1821, the summer semesters of 1823 and 1826, and the winter semester of 1828/1829. There are no existing accounts of the lectures in Heidelberg. The three-volume German text, *Vorlesungen über die Ästhetik*, was compiled by Hegel's student Heinrich Gustav Hotho from Hegel's lecture manuscript (now lost) and student transcripts from the Berlin lecture course. What we have now in two volumes in English is a translation of the text assembled by Hotho and translated by T. M. Knox as *Hegel's Aesthetics: Lectures on Fine Art*. Stephen Houlgate, "Introduction: An Overview of Hegel's Aesthetics," in *Hegel and the Arts* (Evanston, IL: Northwestern University Press, 2007), xii.

8. Hegel, *Aesthetics: Lectures on Fine Art*, 54. Hegel, VA 1: 80–81. Throughout the chapter, in places where I am not directly quoting the English translations, I will replace the term "man" with "human being" or "individual" in order to foster inclusivity of language.

9. . Hegel, *Aesthetics: Lectures on Fine Art*, 53–54.

10. Ibid.

11. Ibid., 54.

12. Hegel, *Aesthetics: Lectures on Fine Art*, 54–55. Hegel, VA 1: 81–82.

13. Hegel, *Aesthetics: Lectures on Fine Art*, 55. Hegel, VA 1: 82. "die Kunst die *Wahrheit* in Form der Sinnlichen Kunstgestaltung zu enthüllen."

14. David Simpson, ed., *The Origins of Modern Critical Thought: German Aesthetic and Literary Criticism from Lessing to Hegel* (Cambridge [England]; New York: Cambridge University Press, 1988), 9.

15. Hegel, *Aesthetics: Lectures on Fine Art*, 66. Hegel, VA 1: 95.

16. Ibid., 64.

17. Ibid., 66. VA 1: 95

18. Ibid., 64. VA 1: 93

19. Ibid., 64–65. VA 1: 93–94.

20. Ibid., 64–65. VA 1: 94.

21. Ibid., 65. VA 1: 94.

22. Jeffrey Reid, *The Anti-Romantic: Hegel Against Ironic Romanticism* (London and New York: Bloomsbury Academic, 2014), 12–13.

23. Hegel, *Aesthetics: Lectures on Fine Art*, 89. Hegel, VA 1: 123.

24. Hegel, *Aesthetics: Lectures on Fine Art*, 11. "In allen diesen Beziehungen ist und bleibt die Kunst nach der Seite ihrer höchsten Bestimmung für uns ein Vergangenes." Hegel, VA 1: 25.

25. Hegel, *Aesthetics: Lectures on Fine Art*, 1236. G. W. F. Hegel, VA 3: 572. "Doch auf diesem Gipfel führt die Komödie zugleich zur Auflösung der Kunst überhaupt."

26. Ibid., 88.

27. In tragedy, the Greek world begins to become aware of its own inner contradictions, and, in this sense, the dissolution that happens in ancient Greek comedy begins already with tragedy.

28. Stephen Houlgate, "Hegel's Theory of Tragedy," in *Hegel and the Arts*, ed. Stephen Houlgate (Evanston, IL: Northwestern University Press, 2007), 155.

29. Stephen C. Law, "Hegel and the Spirit of Comedy: *Der Geist Der Stets Verneint*," in *Hegel and Aesthetics*, ed. William Maker (Albany: State University of New York Press, 2000), 117.

30. Hegel, *Aesthetics: Lectures on Fine Art*, 1206.

31. Hegel, *Aesthetics: Lectures on Fine Art*, 1222.

32. Law, "Hegel and the Spirit of Comedy: Der Geist Der Stets Verneint," 119.

33. Hegel, *Aesthetics: Lectures on Fine Art*, 67. Although I do not develop it here, another way of interpreting the threat that irony poses to Hegel's systematic project (suggested to me by María Acosta) is that irony does not allow for the movement of the dialectic. That is, if we focus on Schlegel's own definition of irony (presented in chapter 1), rather than Hegel's depiction of him in the *Lectures*, it becomes clear that by holding a contradiction (and not allowing for its suspension, cancellation, or sublation), irony is an impediment to *Aufhebung*.

34. Hegel, *Aesthetics: Lectures on Fine Art*, 1222.

35. Another possibility, which Hegel briefly sketches, is that the ironic genius will stop finding satisfaction in his activities of creation and destruction and yearn for something substantial. Hegel, *Aesthetics: Lectures on Fine Art*, 66.

36. Schlegel, *Lucinde and the Fragments*, 146–147. KFSA II, p. 151, CF 37.

37. Ibid.

38. Ibid., 146–147. KFSA II, p. 151, CF 37.

39. KFSA II, 173, AF 53.

40. Schlegel, *Lucinde and the Fragments*, 146. KFSA II, p. 150, CF 33.

41. Novalis, "Novalis, Miscellaneous Observations and Logological Fragments," in *The Bloomsbury Anthology of Aesthetics*, ed. Joseph J. Tanke and Colin McQuillan (Bloomsbury Academic, 2012), p. 315. Logological Fragment 100.

42. Schlegel, *Lucinde and the Fragments*, 144–145. KFSA II, p. 149, CF 20.

43. Michel Chaouli, *The Laboratory of Poetry: Chemistry and Poetics in the Work of Friedrich Schlegel* (Baltimore: Johns Hopkins University Press, 2002), 64.

44. Ibid., 60–61.

45. Friedrich Schlegel, "On Incomprehensibility (1800)," 298. KFSA II, p. 364.

46. Chaouli, *Laboratory of Poetry*, 6. Chaouli clarifies that the conception of chemistry that Schlegel is drawn to is the unstable model of chemistry available at the end of the eighteenth century, just before the atomic model is proposed by Dalton in 1810. Furthermore, because Schlegel does not have a systematic understanding of chemistry (but rather one that Chaouli calls "dilettantish"), he has no obligation to produce a correct account of chemistry. Insofar as Schlegel is not under the constraint to produce an accurate account of chemistry, his aesthetic project actually gets closer to the model of chemistry at the end of the eighteenth century, a model that had chaos and contingency at its heart. Ibid., 2–7.

47. Ibid., 5.

48. Ibid., 4.

49. Ibid., 14.

50. Ibid., 7.

51. Ibid.

52. Ibid.,12.

53. Ibid., 16.

54. Ibid., 11.

55. Judith Norman, "Hegel and Romanticism," in *Hegel and the Arts*, ed. Stephen Houlgate (Evanston, IL: Northwestern University Press, 2007), 318.

56. Schlegel, *Lucinde and the Fragments*, 156. KFSA II, p. 160, CF 108.

57. Eric Miller, "Masks of Negation: Greek Eironeia and Schlegel's Ironie," *ERR European Romantic Review* 8, no. 4 (1997): 360–385.

58. Schlegel, *Lucinde and the Fragments*, 215. KFSA II, 216, AF 344.

59. Ibid., 173. KFSA II, p. 180, AF 99.

60. Ibid., 160. KFSA II, p. 164, Blütenstaub Fragment 20.

61. Ibid., 256, I 156.

62. Ibid., 254. KFSA II, p. 270, I 136.

3

ANOTHER WAY TO THE ABSOLUTE: LANGUAGE AND NAMING IN THE *DAO DE JING*

The striving to know and to communicate the Absolute is an essential feature of romantic philosophy; however, language that describes this striving as moving the knower "toward," "closer," or "nearer" to the Absolute betrays the very methodology of Schlegel's philosophical fragments. These terms emphasize linearity and make it seem as if the Absolute can be reached via an incremental inching toward the whole or through an aggregate of parts. Instead, for Schlegel, the Absolute is approached through an encounter with the ironic fragments. The fragments are non-linear and non-totalizing in both their form and content. Through their form, they point the reader to their incompleteness and to the gaps between them. There is no decisive order in which the fragments must be read and, more importantly, there is no ultimate organization of them that would yield a completed system. As ironic, the fragments introduce a second, equally plausible, meaning and thereby show their reader that her attempts to know are incomplete. The ironic fragments reveal the tension between the desire to communicate fully, i.e., the desire to communicate the whole, and the impossibility of complete communication. However, this tension is not to be overcome, but instead it must be harnessed in the communication of the Absolute. In other words, it is through attending to the role of that which cannot be grasped and exceeds our human endeavors to know that the Absolute can be communicated. In this analysis, these ungraspable elements include incomprehensibility, chaos, and emptiness. Through their fragmentary form, Schlegel's philosophical writings point the reader's attention to what does not appear and remains unknown; furthermore, it is precisely by writing in fragments, rather than attempting to produce a totalizing system, that a realization of the Absolute is possible. Ironically, the whole is communicated through fragments, which immediately proclaim their incompleteness.

Through their form, the ironic fragments present the reader with an implicit critique of philosophy that aims at totalizing; the fragments fulfill this task by attuning their reader to non-presence in a double sense: The fragments point her to the physical spaces between them and to the gaps in what she claims to know. Fragmentation "invites the reader into those gaps" as "a structure that emphasizes what is *unknown* rather than the already articulated known."[1] By gesturing toward what does not appear or what is not known, the ironic fragments offer a critique of a metaphysics of presence. In addition to the implicit critiques launched by the form of the fragments, Schlegel is also explicitly critical of a linear model of progress for philosophy. He writes in *Athenaeum* fragment 43, "Philosophy is still moving too much in a straight line; it's not yet cyclical enough."[2] He describes philosophy using the image of an ellipse in *Ideas* fragment 117, "[the] one center, which we are closer to at present, is the rule of reason [*der Vernunft*]. The other is the idea of the universe, and it is here that philosophy and religion [*der Religion*] intersect."[3] By using this image of a curve with two foci, Schlegel underscores the cyclical nature of philosophy; however, unlike a circle, an ellipse has two foci. In this fragment, Schlegel forecasts a shift in philosophy from reason (its current focus) to religion. As I argued in chapter 1, Schlegel's notion of religion (or re-ligion) can be interpreted to mean the linking of philosophy with other disciplines, in particular with poetry and science. Thus, this shift in focus can be read as a departure from the concern with first principles and completed systems toward romantic philosophy as re-ligion, i.e., as the infinite process of joining disciplines, which begins in the midst of things. This process of linking is already at work in Schlegel's fragments, as well as Novalis' *Romantic Encyclopedia*.

In this chapter, I turn to an ancient Daoist text, the *Dao De Jing*, as a rich resource for how poetic writing can convey a non-linear striving to know the Absolute. Like Schlegel's fragments, the *Dao De Jing* is attuned to the spaces of non-presence, to the cyclical patterns in nature, as well as to the problems encountered when attempts are made to name the whole. I will argue that these two texts, Schlegel's fragments and the *Dao De Jing*, are co-illuminating. The *Dao De Jing* brings into sharper relief how irony and incomprehensibility function in Schlegel's philosophical writings; it offers resources for thinking incomprehensibility as emptiness, in a way that does not attempt to reify either term. Schlegelian irony, in turn, underscores meta-textual issues in the *Dao De Jing*. First, I will briefly address some of the major differences between the two texts. Then, I will examine the following themes in the *Dao De Jing*: 1) the problematic nature of names, 2) the relationship between presence and non-presence, 3) the idea of oneness, 4) the notion of a foundation located at the center, and 5) the principle of dark efficacy. After exploring these central ideas in the context of the *Dao De Jing*, I will highlight some connections between the two texts on these themes and how the intervention of Daoism brings a dynamic concept of the Absolute into sharper relief. Then, before concluding, I will zero in on the privileged position of the individual at the center of each framework: the sage-ruler and the ironic writer.

THE *DAO DE JING*

At the surface level, the romantic fragments and the *Dao De Jing* share in common the fact that they can both be read in any order and have multiple contributing authors. At the deeper level, both texts share a concern with absolute totality, conceived of as the Absolute or the *Dao*, respectively. However, there are some major differences between the two texts in terms of the language and context in which each was composed, as well as their intended audiences. Whereas the ironic fragments are couched within the concerns for German thinkers at the turn of the nineteenth century, the *Dao De Jing* is an ancient Chinese text directed at the ideal ruler during the "warring states period."

The title *Dao De Jing* literally means the "classical scripture" [*Jing*] relating to the Way [*Dao*] and its efficacy [*De*]. The oldest known versions of the text (also called the *Laozi*) were found in excavations in the Chinese provinces of Hunan and Hubei. In the Hunan province, silk manuscripts dating back to 200 BCE were discovered in the tombs of local rulers in 1973. In the latter, Hubei province, bamboo manuscripts, a 100 years older than the silk version, were found in the tombs of aristocrats in 1993.[4] These early versions of the text were not numbered, but simply "flowed"; the later standard versions, edited by Wang Bi, are divided into 81 chapters, with roughly the first half covering the *Dao* and the second half covering *De* (this order was reversed in the earlier versions).[5] The authorship of the text is unknown, but was likely multiple, and some of the chapters include commonly held sayings at the time of the text's composition. However, based on the style of the text, the repetition of "I" as the subject of many passages, and the fact that it was buried in the tombs of aristocrats, it is fairly clear that the intended reader was the singular sage-ruler.

The *Dao De Jing* was composed after the fall of the Western Zhou empire (ca. 1050–771 BCE) during the so-called "warring states period" (475–221 BCE). After the fall of the Zhou Empire, many local principalities cropped up, each attempting to unify the other states under its control. If a state wished to rule all the others, it would need to establish its authority as the rightful heir to the Zhou Empire and provide a political ideology for how unification would be possible.[6] In this context, the *Dao De Jing* reads as an instruction manual for the would-be sage ruler, i.e., the ruler who would unify China. It is a political text, which claims that the model for the state ought to be the harmony humans observe in Nature.[7] A central aim of the text (if it is possible to say such a thing) is to provide instructions for placing human society in harmony with the *Dao*, and thereby ensuring, for humans, the constancy and permanence exemplified by Nature. The *Dao* is not a static unity but rather a dynamic pattern, which includes heaven, earth, and humans; as this dynamic pattern, the *Dao* is also referred to as the ideal scenario. In order to achieve permanence and constancy, or to be in harmony with the ideal scenario, human society must mimic Nature's structure. The ruler plays an important and central role in manifesting order, but this role will be a passive one of doing nothing (as I will elaborate in the following sections). Although the primary aim of the text is political, it also offers metaphysical insights into the nature of the *Dao* itself.

In my analysis, I will primarily be working with the *Dao De Jing*; however, at times, I will refer to another Daoist text composed during the warring states period: the *Zhuangzi*. Because my focus is the *Dao*

De Jing, I will only point to those moments in the *Zhuangzi* that provide a complementary picture of the *Dao*. The *Zhuangzi* is an incredibly rich text and there is much more to say about it than I can do justice to here. The author of the text, Zhuang Zhou (ca. 369–286 BCE), is usually referred to as *Zhuangzi* (master Zhuang). The *Zhuangzi* is comprised of 33 chapters; however, only the first seven chapters (referred to as the "Inner Chapters") are believed by scholars to have actually been composed by Zhuangzi. The remaining chapters, 8 through 22 (the "Outer Chapters") and 23 through 33 (the "Miscellaneous Chapters"), were likely written within 150 years of Zhuangzi's death by multiple authors.[8]

Unlike the claims about the *Dao* in the *Dao De Jing*, which are presented in the context of a political guidebook, the *Zhuangzi* is not explicitly political. Brook Ziporyn recounts an anecdote about Zhuangzi that illustrates his relationship to political office: Reportedly, Zhuangzi said that he would rather wallow in filth than be controlled by any head of state.[9] These two Daoist texts also differ stylistically; whereas, the *Dao De Jing* is comprised of a collection of poetic verses, the *Zhuangzi* proceeds by way of stories about animals, trees, and strange human beings. Sometimes, it presents a dialogue between Zhuangzi and an interlocuter; at other times, the reader is confronted with a series of questions with no apparent answer; the text includes appeals to the wisdom of the ancients, but it is not obvious whether or not these claims are meant to be taken ironically. The *Zhuangzi*'s stories flow one into another; it is not evident where one begins or another ends; the reader may make arbitrary cuts in the text, but the text often resists these divisions by circling back to a story or revealing that what appeared disconnected was perhaps connected after all. The *Zhuangzi* does not present a systematic picture of reality; moreover, it does not even take a position on the truth or falsity of the positions it presents through its characters—the birds, the trees, the discombobulated men—whose perspectives are all equally true (from within themselves). But even to make this latter claim, that perspectivism is the truth (that there is no one true perspective), is to take a position, and therefore the text will not make this claim explicitly. Thus, the text remains silent on this point; or more precisely, it is filled with chatter, but no definitive conclusion.

LANGUAGE AND PARADOX

Rather than offering a definition of the *Dao* (like the one I just provided, at least tentatively, in my opening remarks), the *Dao De Jing's* opening chapter proffers a commentary on the nature of language and the problem with naming:

> As to a Dao—
> If it can be specified as a Dao,
> It is not a permanent Dao.
>
> As to a name—
> If it can be specified as a name,
> It is not a permanent name.[10]

Whatever can be named, set apart, or determined is not really the *Dao* [道].[11] Names are specific and impermanent, whereas the *Dao* is nonspecific and permanent. Names pick out from the whole of reality, whereas the *Dao* is the whole of reality, which includes both what appears (presence) and does not appear (non-presence). When naming, we point out a particular, and in so doing, we determine it as separate from the whole. Thus, the name "*Dao*" betrays what it aims to express by turning the "nonspecific whole" into a particular thing.[12]

The *Dao* is not any particular thing, but every-thing; it is the dynamic whole and the source for the movement and fertility of that whole. Our linguistic expressions betray what we are trying to express; as Novalis puts it, we "thing" that which is no-thing (emptiness) and everything (the whole). If the objective is to name the *Dao*, then it must be named in a way that avoids what naming normally does, i.e., identifying a thing or entity with a specific function or exclusive role, and thus also distinguishing it from what it is not. Although the first chapter of the *Dao De Jing* begins by warning the reader about the problem with naming the *Dao*, i.e., that any *Dao* we can specify is "not a permanent Dao," the text does not simply end there. It proceeds by way of indirect communication through metaphors, paradox, and riddles. The text includes a number of metaphors or images for the *Dao*; throughout this analysis, I will examine the following metaphors: the wheel, the plant, the door or gate, the feminine, the valley, the infant, water, and the uncarved wood. Each of these images conveys a different aspect of the *Dao* while also providing instructions for the sage-ruler.

The metaphor of "uncarved wood" illuminates the meaning of the *Dao* as the "nonspecific whole" while also pointing the reader's attention to the function of names, which will also be their limitation. Chapter 28 of the *Dao De Jing* asserts, "when the carving is begun, then there are names."[13] By describing the *Dao* as "uncarved wood," the text simultaneously refers to it as both everything and no-thing. That is, the uncarved wood is that no-thing (no particular thing) or nothing (emptiness) that can be anything. The *Dao*, as uncarved wood, is the site of unlimited potentiality. Insofar as the uncarved wood is not yet a thing, it can be anything. When the wood is carved up, determinate objects are created and the uncarved wood is restricted. It no longer has the potential to be anything, because it has become one particular thing (or a collection of things). Carving is a metaphor for the process of naming: Names determine the function of an object, and in so doing, limit it. The same goes for the name "*Dao*"; as soon as we name the *Dao*, we specify it and limit it. As soon as we specify it, it is no longer the *Dao*. While the metaphor of the uncarved wood is instructive, it is also contradictory and inadequate; to call that which is uncarved by the name "wood" is to already carve some-thing out from the whole, i.e., to pick out "wood" from other beings. Moreover, the reader is prompted to imagine something, e.g., a block of wood, and thus she objectifies the *Dao* by turning the unthinged into a thing. When the unnameable is named, it is turned into what it is not.

The term *Dao* (typically translated as Way or Course) also functions metaphorically in the text. The Way (or path) is the coincidence of presence and non-presence that allows for walking, or perhaps better yet, the path that is formed in the walking of it.[14] The way or path is a productive metaphor insofar as it conjures up the notion of the space that allows for traveling to happen; this space is no-thing, and depends on its relationship to presence (e.g., gravel or dirt) to be perceived. The metaphor is limited (as are all metaphors), because it causes the reader to imagine a static picture of a walking path, thereby focusing her attention of the aspect of presence, rather than the relationship between presence and non-presence that generates the path. By naming it, the Way—or the permanence of relationality—is transformed into a literal (and thus necessarily impermanent) path.

In addition to metaphor, another technique that is mobilized in the expression of the *Dao* is paradox. For example, chapter 40 of the text states,

> Reversal is the movement of the Dao.
> Weakness is the usefulness of the Dao.
> The things of the world are generated from presence (*you*).
> Presence is generated from nonpresence (*wu*).[15]

Like the wheel's circular movement, the *Dao* returns to its beginning as it advances. The movement of the *Dao* is reversal, and not the linear model for the progress of nature that is often found in the West. This is also why the sage-ruler is compared to an infant; the wise ruler returns to the undifferentiated state at the beginning of life, and it is because the ruler is in this infant-like state, that he has power or efficacy [*de*]. The source for the usefulness of the *Dao* is located in what is conventionally considered weak, rather than what is typically considered strong. In the section on dark efficacy [*de*], I will return to this latter theme with the metaphor of water, which is often viewed as bland and soft, but which can carve out valleys.

PRESENCE AND NON-PRESENCE: THE WHEEL METAPHOR

Chapter 11 of the *Dao De Jing* presents the reader with five metaphors for the *Dao*: the wheel (implicit in the image of the cart), the clay pot, the door, the window, and the room.

> Thirty spokes are united in one hub.
>   It is in the [space of] emptiness,
>   where the usefulness of the cart is.
> Clay is heated and a pot is made.
>   It is in the [space of] emptiness,
>   Where the usefulness of the pot is.
> Doors and windows are chiseled out.
>   It is in its [spaces of] emptiness,
>   where the usefulness of a room is.
> Thus,
>   There is the presence [*you*] for the benefit,
>   there is nonpresence [*wu*] for the use.[16]

What is distinctive about these images is that the source of their utility is the space of non-presence [wu/無]. The clay pot is able to perform its function of holding because its center is empty; it is molded and heated, i.e., determined, in such a way that it is partially left undetermined. Because the space of non-presence is implicit in its structure, it has unlimited possibilities of how it can be filled. Because the doorway is empty, it can fulfill its role of facilitating the movement of people in and out of the room; no matter how often the doorway is used, its emptiness, which allows for its functionality, is never reduced or exhausted. Without its empty center, or hub, the wheel could not be connected to an axle and would not be able to complete the task of turning, which enables the cart to travel. Whereas the clay of the pot or the wood of the spokes will eventually break down and decay, that which is non-material, the emptiness at the heart of each object, is permanent and inexhaustible. My description makes it sound as though emptiness were a thing located at the center of these objects. And, while I have written this way in order to underscore the text's emphasis on emptiness, this language is imprecise insofar as emptiness is no-thing, which is located nowhere. Furthermore, emptiness is singular, i.e., the emptiness at the center of the doorway and the emptiness of the clay pot are one and the same.

I used to live right next to a highway in Chicago, so close, in fact, that a friend once described my view as "drastic." As I wrote this passage on the metaphor of the wheel, I watched the flow of traffic outside my window moving "left and right."[17] My attention was drawn to the trucks passing by. Each has 18 wheels; each wheel has an empty center or hub where the axle is placed so the wheel can turn. The emptiness of the center and the presence of the spokes (in this case the rubber), work together to facilitate the wheel's turning. But the empty center does not *do* anything. Non-action allows for action, i.e., turning, to happen or proceed. This image points to a paradox: Stillness is the source of movement. The wheel cannot turn without the empty center, which does not turn. The empty center is the site of stillness that makes the turning possible. The metaphor of the wheel, as well as the other images in this chapter, underscore the necessity of non-presence for utility. The text emphasizes emptiness; however, non-presence [wu/無] also relies on presence [you/有].[18] Presence and non-presence are co-determining. For example, in the image of the wheel, the hub is only a hub in its relationship to the spokes; outside of this relationship, it does not exist at all. In turn, without the empty center, or the hub, the spokes are merely bits of metal, wood, or rubber. In order to convey its nature (or the nature of Nature), images for the *Dao* have three components: presence (the spokes, in the example of the wheel), non-presence (the empty hub), and the relationship between both presence [*you*/有] and non-presence [*wu*/無], which allows for the turning of the wheel, i.e., the processual nature of Nature.

As an image for the *Dao*, the metaphor of the wheel operates on multiple registers. Chapter 34 says that the *Dao* can be "named with the small" and "mandated with the great."[19] As great, the *Dao* is the entire image of the wheel and its movement, as I described above. However, as small, the *Dao* is the empty center of the wheel that allows it to turn; there is nothing smaller than emptiness. To say that the *Dao* is "small" and "great" is to say that it is simultaneously "nothing" and "no-thing": As the empty center, the *Dao* is nothing, and, as the whole, it is no-thing (no particular thing). Thus, the *Dao* is not only the dynamic whole, but also the source for its movement; it is totality and its creator. But again, the creator is not separate from its creation; this distinction is merely a cut that I have made in order to clarify the structure or pattern of the whole. Robin R. Wang explains, "ambiguity is built into the concept of *Dao*, which is not just the origin but the structure (*ti*) and the functioning (*tong*) of the world, as well as the guide through it."[20] The reference to the small and the great can be read in yet another way: Insofar as the empty center is the source for the movement of the whole, the smallest is the greatest, i.e., the smallest (emptiness) is the greatest because it is the source for the whole. That which is nothing and the source for every-thing is simultaneously "small" and "great."

The text's emphasis on emptiness, especially in the wheel metaphor, is also connected to its political message and its intended audience: The would-be sage-ruler. In the image of the wheel, the spokes represent the people; like spokes, each individual is equidistant from the ruler. Just as a wheel does not turn smoothly if the spokes are not of an equal length and distance from the hub, the societal wheel would not turn smoothly if the ruler favored any of his subjects. The ruler's indifference allows the smooth and harmonious flow of society. Indifference is one way of describing the ruler's emptiness. The ruler is also empty, or hub-like, insofar as he is impartial, without desire, and practices non-speaking and inaction [*wu wei*]. Because the ruler does not have a specific function, this also means that the ruler does not have a name, since names designate function.[21] Just as the stillness of the hub allows the turning of the wheel to happen, by not acting, the sage allows the citizens (i.e., the spokes) to perform their tasks in a self-so [*ziran*] manner. The language of "allowing" is crucial here; the hub does not force the wheel to turn, and likewise the ruler does not coerce the citizens into doing their tasks; instead, the sage-ruler empties himself out so that the citizens can perform their roles in a self-so or spontaneous manner. Wang explains the role of the *Dao* as spontaneity or *ziran* with reference to chapter 25 of the *Dao De Jing*; there, humans follow the earth as their guide, the earth follows heaven (sky), heaven follows the *Dao*, but the *Dao* is self-so [*ziran*]. If the *Dao* was not "so of itself," an infinite regress would occur.[22] To be in harmony with *Dao* means that society would function in a self-so manner, i.e., the wheel would turn without any external force or coercion. The sage is a not a typical ruler; he does not force the people to perform their tasks, but rather by doing nothing, he creates the conditions for spontaneity to occur.

DAO AS ONENESS

As the pattern that generates and ties together heaven, earth, and human beings, the *Dao* can be conceived as oneness. Robin R. Wang expresses it thus, "[the] world is not constructed from individual pieces, but rather is an indivisible whole taking patterns and processes of interrelatedness as its fundamental structure."[23] A well-known image for oneness, which is referenced in the *Dao De Jing*, but which predates it, is *yinyang*. *Yinyang* is represented by an image of a circle composed of two halves: one black (*yin*) and one white (*yang*). *Yin* represents night, darkness, and the feminine, whereas *yang* represents day, light and the masculine. Although *yin* and *yang* seem like static concepts, they do not refer to any particular thing, but rather to phenomena—"the interplay between the sun, a hill, and the light."[24] *Yinyang* is a description of the hill as the sun passes over in the sky. The sunny side of the hill is *yang* and the shady side is *yin*; *yinyang* is thus both relational and contextual. Each aspect of *yinyang*—light and dark—is impermanent on its own; however, constancy is born out of their relationship, i.e., out of the permanent pattern of light and dark. This pattern of night and day or black and white is called the "world's pattern." As the "world's pattern," *yinyang* is conceived as oneness; however, seen in their distinction from one another, *yin* and *yang* form a binary opposition. Threeness emerges when we have the agility to think twoness (Fduality) alongside oneness (unity). The agile mind, to borrow Schlegel's term, is the mind that can quickly shift between the equally true perspectives of oneness, twoness and threeness; ultimately, this mind could hold multiple positions, without choosing one or disregarding their differences.

The relationship between "oneness" and "twoness" is expressed in the *Zhuangzi* with regard to the issue with naming. Our objective is to describe the *Dao* as "oneness," but as soon as we name it "oneness," we create two: the oneness itself and the word "oneness." In this quickly multiplying process of naming, twoness, turns into threeness: the oneness itself, the word "oneness," and that which still remains unnamed.[25] Naming is the process by which we cut up the world; therefore, if our intention is to reach "oneness," carving up the world will never get us there—the more we cut, the further we are from the "oneness" we aim to express. Moreover, there is always something that remains unnamed, or uncut, in the process. The *Zhuangzi* offers an alternative to carving up the world in a passage from the second Inner Chapter. The text refers to the ancients as an exemplar, because their understanding had gotten "all the way there"; to get "all the way there" means that there are no things, and when there are no things, nothing can be added.[26] Elaborating the path from the ancients to our situation, Zhuangzi tells the reader that there were those for whom things existed but without definite boundaries; then, those for whom there were boundaries, but no sense of right or wrong; finally, there were those for whom "rights and wrongs waxed bright," and when this was the case "the Course began to wane."[27] Here, the Course is a translation for *Dao*. To get all the way there, as the ancients had, is for there to be no things and no divisions at all. The next best, so it seems from the list, is to have divisions but without definite boundaries; implicitly definite boundaries would be worse than indefinite ones. Finally, having definite boundaries with corresponding rights and wrongs would be the worst situation and the one that we currently find ourselves, i.e., the situation where the Course is waning. The text is describing a situation of oneness without words, without labels, and without things; this is the uncarved wood of the *Dao De Jing*. However, at least ostensibly, the text is offering a procedure for securing this understanding of the ancients if we follow its description in reverse order. I say ostensibly, because immediately after detailing this procedure, the speaker asks whether waning and fullness can be distinguished; thereby, in an ironic gesture similar to Schlegel's in "On Incomprehensibility," he undermines the very same procedure he just layed out. Another passage in the same Inner Chapter describes this scenario of oneness: "Nothing in the world is larger than the tip of a hair in autumn, and Mt. Tai is small. No one lives longer than a dead child, and old Pengzu died an early death. Heaven and earth are born together with me, and the ten thousand things and I are one."[28] True oneness implies a situation where there is no division between an "I" and oneness. As soon as "I" emerge, a cut is made and oneness is split into two. As I continue the process of cutting up the world, I move further away from the oneness I set out to describe.

Although these descriptions of forgetting divisions imply a state without words, they appear within a text, which, as such, must utilize language; this means that the text must wield language skillfully so that it does not simply create a situation where "rights and wrongs [wax] bright." Given the emphasis on forgetting in this and other passages, it seems that knowing the Way is different than our usual ways of understanding (i.e., the thin watered-down type of reason in Schlegel). In chapter 48 of the *Dao De Jing*, the text expresses a similar relationship to the *Dao* when it says, "One who engages in learning/ increases daily/ One who hears the Dao/diminishes daily."[29] Knowing the *Dao* is not a matter of accumulation; rather, it is a process of unlearning, emptying oneself out, or becoming hub-like. In chapter 26 of the *Zhuangzi's* Miscellaneous Chapters, the role of language is conveyed ironically. The text draws a comparison between traps (e.g., for fish or rabbits) and words; whereas the fish trap is used to capturing fish, words are traps for capturing intent. In the case of the fish trap, its user can forget the trap once she has caught the fish; likewise the text says, "[When] you have got hold of the intent, you forget the words." But the passage does not end with the forgetting of words. Rather, immediately after this last claim it asks, "[Where] can I find a man who has forgotten words, so I can have a few words with him?"[30] The last sentence is crucial, because it transforms the passage into an ironic utterance. That is, the goal seems to be to forget words, but the speaker ends by asking where he can find someone who has forgotten words so he can have a few words with him—but how can you speak to the one who has forgotten words? And, on the meta-textual level, how can the one who has forgotten words write about this forgetting?

In the *Dao De Jing*, the theme of oneness not only emerges with the image of *yinyang* and the problem with naming, but also through the metaphors for the creative activity of Nature. The text paints a fully immanent picture in which the creator and creation are one.

> The ten thousand things occur along with each other:
> So I watch where they turn.
> The things of the world are manifold,
>   they all return again to their root:
>   "stillness."[31]

This chapter, written from the perspective of the sage-ruler, brings together the images of the wheel and the roots of the plant. In the first half of the quote, the hub of the wheel, or the axis, is the site from which the ruler can observe the way of the 10,000 things (or all the beings of the world). This axis point, or empty center, can also be interpreted as the *Dao* as the source for all beings, which allows for the flow of nature. The second half of the quote evokes the image of the plant and its root structure. The *Dao*, as source, is the root structure; the roots are the dark, hidden and still source for the plant's growth. The plant metaphor emphasizes the co-emergence of the *Dao* as creator with its creation. The roots are not, as Hans-Georg Moeller emphasizes, an origin that is separate from its creation, as in the Western Christian tradition's conception of a transcendent God.[32] Rather, the roots and the plant co-emerge and are co-extensive with one another: As the plant grows upward into presence, the roots grow deeper into the dark earth. In the images of the wheel and the plant, the creative source is not separate from what it generates: The hub is located at the center of the wheel and the roots are part of the overall structure of the plant. Although not visible, each aspect is the source for the movement and productivity of the whole.

FOUNDATION AT THE CENTER

Because emptiness is quite literally at the center of the images employed throughout the *Dao De Jing*, the text avoids the Western predilection to think foundationally about emptiness or incomprehensibility as something to be overcome in order for thinking and communication to take place. Rather, emptiness or incomprehensibility is a necessary part of the processes of conceiving and communicating the whole. Not only is emptiness a necessary part of the whole, but it is a part that generates the functionality of the whole: The empty hub enables the wheel to turn, the hollow center of the cup makes drinking possible, and the space inside the frame of the door allows for the entering and exiting of a room. Emptiness is at the heart of the images used to describe the *Dao*. Emptiness is a necessary part of the whole, but one that cannot be conceptualized, held, or contained by structures of human knowing; strictly speaking, it is nothing. To write *about* "emptiness" betrays the very thing we aim to communicate; emptiness is reified into a static concept and objectified; nothing is turned into something. Therefore, a text that wishes to communicate emptiness, without in the process objectifying it, must perform it. In the *Dao De Jing*, emptiness is not only a component of the metaphors it presents to its reader, but also a crucial aspect of the text itself, which lends to its mysterious and cryptic quality. Insofar as the text itself is empty at its heart, it eludes our grasping for it and resists any attempts to comprehend it fully. Take the earlier example of the metaphor of uncarved wood: This phrase is contradictory and ungraspable. To introduce the word "wood" is already to begin the process of carving up the *Dao* and thus abandon its nature as uncarved. Or, the line I quoted earlier from chapter 40, which states, "presence is generated from nonpresence." But, how can this be? How can something come from nothing? How can "*wu*/無" generate "*you*/有"? Just as the empty center of the wheel facilitates the wheel's turning, the emptiness at the center of this text allows it to remain dynamic. Emptiness is ungraspable and therefore an empty text cannot be fully grasped or comprehended by its reader. As Schlegel says of Socratic irony, "it will remain riddle even after it is openly confessed."[33] The *Dao De Jing* not only describes, via images, a vision of the *Dao* that emphasizes the procession of the whole through the relationship between non-presence and presence, but also performs this very movement with the reader through the emptiness at the heart of the text itself.

DARK EFFICACY

> Know the masculine and maintain the feminine—
> > be the world's river
> Be the world's river
> > and constant efficacy won't leave you.³⁴

The rest of chapter 28 of the *Dao De Jing* repeats the structure of this first stanza. The verses therein direct the sage-ruler to be the "world's valley" and the "world's pattern" in order to maintain efficacy [*de*]. In each couplet, the sage-ruler is instructed to know both aspects of each binary, but to maintain the *yin* aspect, i.e., the aspect that is dark, hidden, or lies below. Although constancy is born out of the relationship of *yin* and *yang*, i.e., out of the permanent pattern of night and day, the ordinary people tend to focus their attention on the *yang* aspect of Nature. That is, it is conventional to focus on presence, activity, tasks, and names. It is the task of the sage-ruler to embody the *yin* aspect in order for the constant flow of Nature to proceed in a self-so [*ziran*] or spontaneous manner. In order to ensure the spontaneous (self-so) flow of society, the wise ruler takes the role that no one else wants, i.e., the role of no role. The ruler's role is conveyed through the images of the river, the valley, and the feminine; each of these images emphasizes the practice of taking the lowest place.

The ruler's low position is conveyed through the text's repetition of water images. Water lacks agency; it merely flows to the lowest place. Water lacks shape; it takes on the shape of whatever container it finds itself in. It is precisely the qualities that make water seem bland and weak that allow it to "run over" or erode that which is typically considered hard.³⁵ Water is an exemplar of dark efficacy in nature. Dark efficacy is a reversal of the conventional meaning of power, i.e., the weak defeats the strong and the soft overcomes the hard. Since this type of power is not conventionally practiced (and cannot technically be "practiced" since it is a form of inaction), the text relies on examples in nature for this model of rulership.

Along the same lines, the ruler is instructed to take on the qualities of the valley and the feminine. Because the valley lies low, water flows there; the space of non-presence allows the valley to be a location for the lush growth of vegetation. The valley and the feminine point to emptiness as the site for the potency and generative capacity of nature. The image of the feminine operates in at least two ways. The womb can represent the generative nature of Nature; the womb is that empty space that allows for the growth of the embryo. Invoking the feminine is also a way of instructing the ruler to take the lower position, like the valley. As Moeller explains, the text uses traditional Chinese characters for masculine and feminine that typically refer to animals; therefore, the text is referring to the "sexual aspect of nature" in which the female takes the "lower position" since "[fluids] and water flow downwards, so the absorbing position is the one that lies low."[36] Like water, which flows to the lowest place, the feminine is the aspect that lies below; however, this "lower position" is the source of the strength of the feminine aspect of nature. In other places in the text, the metaphor of the feminine is employed in a more overtly political context; for example, in chapter 61, the large state is instructed to lie below the small state in order to absorb it.

The metaphor of the plant also repeats the instructions for the sage to assume the *yin* aspect. The roots are the part of the plant's overall structure, which remains buried in the dark earth; yet, that which lies below is the source for the growth and maturation of the plant. Non-presence is the source for presence. In each image, the source (or even creator) is part of the structure of its creation, but it is a source that stays hidden or lies below. Given these instructions, the reader can infer that the ruler who follows the *Dao De Jing* as a handbook will not stand before large audiences and give grand speeches. This atypical ruler is the one who stays hidden and practices non-action and non-speaking.

ROMANTIC CONNECTIONS

I will now examine the fruits of this encounter with Daoism. The early German romantics and the Daoists share a common concern with language and the problem of naming. Novalis beautifully captures the difficultly of trying to capture the Absolute with words in the Pollen fragment that I quoted in the introduction: "Everywhere we seek the unthinged [*das Unbedingte*] and find only things [*nur Dinge*]."[37] Linguistic conceptualizations necessarily reify that which they attempt to know. Concepts transform whatever they seek to know into an object that they can grasp. This relationship between concepts and grasping is even clearer in the German word for concept, *Begriff*, which is derived from the verb "to grasp" [*begreifen*]. In order to communicate the "unthinged," language must be used against its propensity to merely grasp.

Similarly, the *Dao De Jing* expresses the problem with naming the *Dao*. The *Dao* is the "nonspecific whole" and the permanent pattern, but names are, by their nature, specific and impermanent. In addition to alerting the reader to the problem with names, the text also demonstrates methods for communicating the whole, which do not reify its dynamic movement. In order to avoid objectifying the *Dao*, language must be used skillfully. The *Zhuangzi* tells the story of Cook Ding who has never needed to sharpen his blade even after years of cutting up oxen. Cook Ding's blade has never dulled, because he places it into the empty space that already exists in the joints.[38] In the *Dao De Jing*, examples of the skillful use of the blade—which enters into the empty spaces—include metaphor and paradox; these techniques do not hack at the world, but rather they attend to the necessary spaces of emptiness.

By reading Schlegelian irony in conversation with the *Dao De Jing* and the *Zhuangzi*, an interpretation of irony emerges that is attuned to the role of non-presence and emptiness. Like Cook Ding's skillful relationship to empty space, irony's form creates the space for contradictory ideas to dwell together. Irony is the force that allows the mind to hold two contradictory thoughts together without diluting either or conflating one into the other. Our usual ways of comprehending the world only let us grasp one side of a binary opposition at a time, whereas irony is the form that allows for the holding of both sides of a contradiction.

The *Dao De Jing* elaborates an unconventional type of power [*de*], which is often overlooked; this power or efficacy is dark and hidden; it appears in forms that are not typically perceived to be strong (such as water). Dark efficacy is the harnessing of the power of passivity, of lying low, of not doing and not speaking. It is counterintuitive to humans, but nature models its influence. The idea of dark efficacy [*de*] from the *Dao De Jing* is at work in Schlegel's philosophy in a couple of ways. First, in his essay "On Incomprehensibility," Schlegel defends incomprehensibility and chaos; he identifies both elements as what remains hidden but is necessary to the structures of human knowing. In the essay, Schlegel is critical of attempts to fully comprehend the world, to fit everything into the structures of human understanding, or to bring everything to light. Although Schlegel compliments those artistic creations of human beings, namely all the structures of meaning, he points our attention to what lies outside those structures as their complement that cannot be grasped. Because, according to Schlegel, the structures of meaning are created by the understanding out of incomprehensibility or chaos, this means that if we scrutinize them intently enough, we will reach "something" not comprehensible, which nonetheless serves as the "basis" for those structures. Again, the language of basis, thing, and outside are problematic; they betray the aim of the text. Schlegel is describing that which has not yet been comprehended or is still in a "state" of chaos, which means it cannot be labeled as being a foundation or squarely outside the structures of the understanding.

To further draw out the connection between Schlegel's account of incomprehensibility or chaos and the metaphors in the *Dao De Jing*, the empty space, for Schlegel, is that which lies "outside" the realm of human understanding and eludes our grasping for it. Schlegel describes that which shores up the burden of our structures of meaning as in the "dark"; like many of the images in the *Dao De Jing* (such as the roots of the plant), that which is hidden makes possible the utility of what we see. Irony—perhaps even the irony of this very passage from Schlegel's essay—gestures toward what we cannot know, to the empty space necessary for any knowing to happen, without, at the same time, grasping it and thus doing violence to that which "supports the entire burden." The *Dao De Jing* shows its reader that this support can be found at the center. Indeed, irony is a central component of Schlegel's philosophical method, which reveals the unsaid in the midst of the said. This latter claim is connected to the second way that irony's efficacy [*de*] is dark: Irony does not directly attempt to communicate the whole. By pointing out an absence in what we know, through undercutting our efforts to grasp the whole, irony actually brings us closer to the whole, which is the dynamic relationship between presence and non-presence, between that which is and which is not, or between what we know and what exceeds our understanding. Irony indirectly reveals that which is present in its absence. Irony, as the *form* of paradox, allows for the holding of two conflicting ideas but is itself neither of them. Like the utility of emptiness in the images of the *Dao De Jing*, irony *allows* for the holding of contradictory ideas, but is, strictly speaking, no-thing.

As a metaphor for the *Dao*, the wheel emphasizes the cyclical nature of Nature and provides resources for thinking about Schlegel's claim that philosophy is still too linear. The metaphor of the wheel emphasizes circular movement without beginning or end; this movement relies on both presence and non-presence in order to proceed. Within the image of the wheel (as well as *yinyang*), the reader also gets a picture of the complementarity of opposing forces that compose the whole: *Yin* and *yang* are relational concepts, non-presence and presence rely upon each other, emptiness and fullness constitute each other. Non-presence is not to be overcome, but it is the source for the movement of the whole. In the *Dao De Jing*, the reader encounters the notion of a source, which is fully immanent. This idea is illustrated through the empty hub at the center of the wheel and through the roots of the plant, which are part of the structure of the plant. In other words, the *Dao* (or Absolute) is not transcendent, nor is it not separate from the knowing subject, which means the ordinary uses of the understanding that try to inch toward it can never succeed.

The wheel is also an image for conceiving of the romantic imperative to join disciplines. Each spoke represents a different field, such as philosophy, art, poetry, chemistry, biology, psychology, politics, mathematics, or mineralogy. As spokes are added, our attention is now drawn to the space between the new spokes, which represent the possibility for misunderstanding as additional disciplines are joined together. The image is limited insofar as it seems like we could eliminate any space by simply adding enough spokes; however, in the case of knowledge, the pursuit is endless, since the whole cannot be achieved through accumulation, i.e., as no-thing it cannot be reached through an aggregate of things. And, because, as Schlegel says, "[ignorance] increases in the same proportion as knowledge—or rather, not ignorance, but knowledge of ignorance."[39] Moreover, the conversation with Daoism brings into sharper relief the necessity of emptiness for the dynamic activity of philosophizing, which occurs through the continued joining of disciplines.

SAGE-RULER AND IRONIST

Before concluding, I turn briefly to the individual located at the center of each text, the sage-ruler and the ironic writer, particularly in terms of the role of indifference and non-mastery for each. Addressing the sage-ruler and the use of paradoxical language in the *Dao De Jing*, Moeller reads the opening lines of chapter 2 as ironical (and I would argue his operating definition of irony is the same as Schlegel's):

> Everybody in the world knows the beautiful as being beautiful.
>   Thus there is already ugliness.
> Everybody knows what is good.
> Thus there is that which is not good.[40]

Moeller argues, however, that only the Daoist sage can "equally appreciate the two moments as equally constitutive of reality or of the movement of the Dao."[41] Although the judgments of beauty and ugliness are opposed, both are necessary for the activity of judging as such to be possible. The sage is the one who is able to take the position of indifference; from this position, he realizes that both attitudes are equally important for communication to take place and to continue.[42] As hub-like, the sage is emptied of self and located in an equal position to each of the spokes; because of this relationship (which is really no relationship at all), he is indifferent to the particular spokes. The spokes could represent judgments such as beauty, ugliness, good, and not good (as in the verses quoted above); or, they could represent different people, seasons, or viewpoints. Ideally, the sage's indifference would be so thoroughgoing that he would not even be partial to the human over the animal, plant, or mineral.

The sage's emptiness is also expressed in terms of his uselessness, or in other words, his mastery of non-mastery. His uselessness is what allows him to be great. The Daoist ruler is the one who masters non-mastery and thus can never be mastered or ruled.

> "only since I master nothing
> no one masters me."[43]

Because the sage reveres words and actions, he uses them sparingly. Thus, the sage-ruler practices non-action and non-speaking. To master the sage's words is a simple task, insofar as there are very few words (or ideally no words); however, no one else in the world does this. The latter statement has two possible meanings: 1) Inaction is not conventionally practiced; 2) to have no task entails having no name, which means, strictly speaking, that the one who does nothing is no one.

Non-mastery is a form of dark efficacy; because the ruler masters nothing, he cannot be ruled by anyone else. On the contrary, if someone is skilled at a particular task, for example playing the violin, it will always be possible for someone else to outperform that person. The same goes for any type of knowledge viewed as an accumulation; no matter how much you know about a topic, say Romanticism or Daoism, there will always be someone who knows more than you. However, it is impossible to know more about knowing nothing or to outperform anyone at doing nothing. Emptiness cannot be made more or less; it cannot be done better or worse.[44] Like the hub of the wheel, emptiness is always singular. The hub of the wheel is also that aspect of the wheel which, as nothing, is, strictly speaking, useless; however, without the hub, the wheel could not turn. By doing nothing, the ruler allows the societal wheel to turn smoothly, and thus, his uselessness is also his greatness.[45]

For the ironic writer (and, by extension, the ironic reader), the indifference of the sage is reflected in the capacity to hold both sides of a contradiction without preference. Ironic texts train the reader's mind to see from the different viewpoints of the various spokes, i.e., to observe the 10,000 things from the axis-point. The indifference of the hub to the spokes is not the negative picture of indifference painted by Hegel when he criticizes Schlegel as the divine ironic genius. This is not distance from the earth that flattens out everything beneath the divine ironic genius, thereby deflating its value and making it insubstantial. Rather, indifference allows the individual at the axis-point to hold multiple viewpoints simultaneously and thus brings her nearer, not further, from the truth as the whole. Indifference is the source for irony's power [*de*]. This ironic stance is also not a position that entails mastery, but rather, it is characterized by the mastery of non-mastery. Non-mastery leaves space for that which cannot be known, and in so doing, brings the ironical-sage into contact with the Absolute.

CONCLUSION

The *Dao De Jing* begins by instructing the reader about the problem with names, i.e., that which can be named is not really the *Dao*. However, the text *proceeds* by providing a number of metaphors for the *Dao*. In order to describe the *Dao* and to instruct the sage on the appropriate way to rule for maintaining stability and harmony, the text's metaphors underscore the role of emptiness, non-presence, and uselessness. In these images of natural and artificial objects, the source of the utility of each object is the space of non-presence. The clay pot is able to perform its function of holding because its center is empty; the wheel is able to turn because of its empty hub; the valley is the location for growth of vegetation because it is empty and lies low. On its own, the empty space is useless, but relationally, it is necessary for the usefulness of each entity. Additionally, the image of the wheel demonstrates that what lies outside human knowing can be located in the center, and indeed that it does play a central role; by doing nothing, the empty hub allows for the smooth turning of the wheel. The *Dao De Jing* presents a model for philosophizing that does not rely on notions of linear progress, but rather underscores the role of the cyclical, i.e., that to proceed can mean a return to the beginning, to a state of undifferentiated potentiality.

Reading the *Dao De Jing* through the unlikely lens of Schlegel's definition of irony encourages the reader to see the necessity of its style. If the reader approaches this cryptic text with the aim of comprehending its meaning, she will inevitably be frustrated and disappointed. Some passages sound like riddles, many seem overly vague, paradoxes multiply but never resolve. However, we can still analyze the text's use of metaphors and paradox in order to articulate how it performs the relationship between the *Dao* and the reader through the process of poetic mysticism. Implicit to the structure of the *Dao De Jing* are the ways that it resists the reader's attempts to grasp its meaning; and, insofar as the text resists the reader's attempts to master it, it brings her closer to the whole, which, like the image of the wheel, must include that which is no-thing but is generative of all things. On a meta-textual level, the *Dao De Jing*, much like the images it provides, contains empty spaces. It is not fully digestible or graspable by its reader. The text performs the content of its message at the level of its form. The verses, like the *Dao*, remain mysterious. The center of the text is empty.

The dialogue with Daoism also highlights the way in which Schlegel's philosophical project undermines a metaphysics of presence, i.e., the ironic fragments point us toward the role of non-presence, to the gaps in our understanding, and to what exceeds the human. However, this does not mean that non-presence (what is unsaid or unknown) ought to be overcome; rather it is integral to the movement of the whole. The agile thinker does not merely try to understand the world by cutting it apart, but rather she has a sense for that which can only be felt and exceeds all her attempts to know. Schlegel's fragments and the *Dao De Jing* subvert a relationship to texts that would aim at mastery. Because both these texts contain gaps and empty spaces, their meanings cannot be exhausted by their readers. Dark efficacy denotes a counterintuitive notion of strength, i.e., the strength of what is conventionally considered weak. Like the sage who cannot be mastered because he is empty and masters nothing, these texts cannot be grasped because of their emptiness; and, in this resistance to being mastered, they offer the reader more.

These two texts use language against itself, through the poetic techniques of irony and paradox, to gain access to that which is not masterable without at the same time mastering it. Rather than seeking to grasp, comprehend, or encompass the whole, they use language against itself in order to convey the whole without breaking it apart or applying categories that would attempt to contain it. Furthermore, by not overcoming the empty space—the incomprehensible or that which lies outside the human—they actually bring their respective readers in contact with the whole (the Absolute for Schlegel, the *Dao* in the *Dao De Jing*). I will continue this analysis of how poetic texts facilitate an intuition of the whole through the relationship with their reader in the next chapter, where I analyze John Ashbery's *Flow Chart*. Ashbery's poem exhibits dark efficacy by harnessing the power of what is typically considered extraneous to the work of art. Through the power of monotony and "extra material," a wave-like movement is generated: The text's meaning approaches and recedes from the reader offering her an intuition of the whole.

NOTES

1. Brenda Miller and Suzanne Paola, *Tell It Slant: Writing and Shaping Creative Nonfiction*, 1st ed. (Boston: McGraw-Hill Humanities, 2003), 147.
2. Schlegel, *Lucinde and the Fragments*, 166. AF 43.
3. Ibid., 252. KFSA II, p. 267, I 117.
4. Hans-Georg Moeller, *Daoism Explained: From the Dream of the Butterfly to the Fishnet Allegory* (Open Court, 2011), 2-3.
5. Moeller, *Daoism Explained*, 2.
6. Brook Ziporyn, "Introduction," in *Zhuangzi: The Essential Writings with Selections from Traditional Commentaries* (Hackett Publishing, 2009), xii.
7. When I capitalize "Nature," I use it as a name for the entire dynamic pattern, which includes heaven (or sky), earth and humans. When I employ "nature," in contrast, I am referring to the term's meaning as the basic inherent features of something. By the phrase, "the nature of Nature," I refer to the inherent qualities or patterns of the whole.
8. Ziporyn, "Introduction," ix.
9. Ibid., vii.
10. Hans-Georg Moeller, trans., *Dao De Jing (Laozi): A Complete Translation and Commentary* (Chicago and La Salle, IL: Open Court, 2007), 3.
11. When capitalized, *"Dao"* refers to the perfect scenario (or Way), which includes human society, earth, and heaven, and which constantly flows. This perfect scenario is the singular pattern of all patterns, rather than a particular scenario or pattern for a specific action. The term *"dao"* without the capitalization refers to "ways" in the plural, e.g., the *dao* of warfare, the *dao* of governing, the *dao* of cooking, and so on. Strictly speaking, these two senses of the singular or plural *Dao/dao* cannot be separated; the *Dao* is the pattern expressed in all these other patterns (*daos*).
12. "Commentary on Chapter One," in Moeller, trans., *Dao De Jing (Laozi)*, 5. I am indebted to Hans Georg-Moeller's translation and commentary of the *Dao De Jing*. I borrow his expression "nonspecific whole" to describe the *Dao* from his commentary to the first chapter of the *Dao De Jing*.
13. Moeller, trans., *Dao De Jing (Laozi)*, 79.
14. The earliest characters for *Dao* depict a head covered by a cloth while walking, or a head walking on a winding road. Thus, the *Dao* has a twofold meaning corresponding to the two characters: 1) The road or path upon which one walks; and 2) guidance, in terms of the path we follow when lost. Robin R. Wang, *Yinyang: The Way of Heaven and Earth in Chinese Thought and Culture* (Cambridge University Press, 2012), 44–45.
15. Ibid., 97.
16. Ibid., 27.

17. Ibid., 83.

18. "*you*/有" and "*wu*/無" are often translated, respectively, as presence/non-presence, or being/non-being; however, literally they mean "to have" and "to lack" (usually "to have" or "to lack" something). Wang, *Yinyang*, 56

19. Moeller, trans., *Dao De Jing (Laozi)*, 83.

20. Wang, *Yinyang*, 47.

21. Throughout, I have retained the masculine pronouns when referring to the sage-ruler. Given the context in which the *Dao De Jing* was written, it is pretty safe to assume that the ruler would be a man; however, given this analysis and the fact that the ruler has no name and no function, it does not really make sense to consider the ruler as gendered. Moreover, the ruler does not have the qualities of the ordinary people, nor does "he" even have any preference for the human (over the heavenly or earthly).

22. Wang, *Yinyang*, 53–54.

23. Wang, *Yinyang*, 48.

24. Wang, *Yinyang*, 24. For a fuller account of the concept of *yinyang*, I highly recommend this illuminating text by Robin R. Wang. I have opted for Wang's spelling of the term as "*yinyang*," which emphasizes the dynamic relationship, rather than separation, of the two terms.

25. Zhuangzi, *Zhuangzi: The Essential Writings*, 16.

26. Ibid., 14.

27. Ibid., 14–15.

28. Ibid., 15.

29. Moeller, trans., *Dao De Jing (Laozi)*, 115.

30. Zhuangzi, *Zhuangzi: The Essential Writings*, 114.

31. Moeller, trans., *Dao De Jing (Laozi)*, 41.

32. Ibid., 52.

33. Schlegel, *Lucinde and the Fragments*, 155–156. KFSA II, p. 160, CF 108.

34. Moeller, trans., *Dao De Jing (Laozi)*, 71.

35. Ibid., 105.

36. "Commentary on Chapter 61," in Moeller, trans., *Dao De Jing (Laozi)*, 140.

37. Novalis, *Philosophical Writings*, trans. Margaret Mahoney Stoljar (Albany: State University of New York Press, 1997), 23.

38. Zhuangzi, *Zhuangzi: The Essential Writings*, 22.

39. Schlegel, *Lucinde and the Fragments*, 200, AF 267.

40. Moeller, trans., *Dao De Jing (Laozi)*, 7.

41. Moeller, *The Philosophy of the Daodejing*, 104.

42. Ibid., 105.

43. Moeller, trans., *Dao De Jing (Laozi)*, 163.

44. In this passage, there is a play on the word *zhi* [知], which can mean "to master," "to know (how)," or "to rule." "Commentary on Chapter Seventy," in Moeller, trans., *Dao De Jing (Laozi)*, 62.

45. The connection between uselessness and greatness is also repeated throughout the stories in the *Zhuangzi's* Inner Chapters. Some of the stories describe enormous trees; because these trees cannot be leveled or cut down, they are deemed useless by conventional standards, in particular by the carpenter. Insofar as they are useless, nothing is able to harm them, and they are able to live out their natural life spans. This connection between uselessness and avoiding harm is also mirrored in the descriptions of the sage-ruler in the *Dao De Jing*.

4

HOW TO READ A RIVER: POETIC MYSTICISM IN JOHN ASHBERY'S *FLOW CHART*

In his fourth Critical fragment, Schlegel writes that there are plenty of fragments, sketches and raw materials, but "there is nothing more rare than a poem!"[1] From this statement, the reader is prompted to infer a contrast between the poem and the other materials just named; that is, if the poem is not merely a draft and if it is not fragmentary, then it must be complete unto itself. In this fragment about fragmentary writings, Schlegel employs the poem as a stand-in for the Absolute. In this chapter, I will argue that John Ashbery's *Flow Chart* (1991) is a poem in this latter sense. Ashbery's poem performs absoluteness as a dynamic movement through its relationship with its reader. *Flow Chart*'s movements, which require the reader in order to be set into motion, give rise to an intuition of the whole. An analysis of *Flow Chart* and of Ashbery's writing style reveals the textual nature of the striving toward the Absolute. In addition, through this dialogue with Ashbery's poetry, Schlegel's conception of the Absolute is brought into sharper relief.

During his lifetime, John Ashbery won almost every major American award for poetry; he was a member of the New York School of poetry and is considered to be one of the greatest poets of the twentieth century. My intention is not to revise the historical record by making a case for including Ashbery among the romantic circle. Given the expansiveness of the ideal of romantic poetry established in *Athenaeum* 116 and this ideal's emphasis on the marriage of philosophy and poetry, it would be easy enough to make such a case. Rather, what I propose to show is that Ashbery's poem *Flow Chart* achieves the aim of romantic striving: an intuition of the Absolute. Following some general remarks regarding the poem's origin, style, and possible interpretations, I will elaborate some points of connection between the works of Schlegel and Ashbery in terms of four central themes in each: 1) Incomprehensibility, 2) systematicity, 3) genius, and 4) the relationship to the reader.

THE POEM

According to the stories about *Flow Chart*'s inception, Ashbery's artist friend Trevor Winkfield challenged him to write a 100-page poem about his deceased mother in 100 days, or by Ashbery's sixtieth birthday.[2] The result of this challenge is *Flow Chart*, a book-length poem comprised of 4,794 lines, which are further divided into six numbered sections (added later by Ashbery). In its origins, the poem is already relational; it is a response to an invitation from his friend. This invitation, in turn, is relative to the recent passing of Ashbery's mother. Contingency not only plays a crucial role in the poem's origins, but, as I will argue in the section on genius, Ashbery's writing style creates openings that enable the poem to be infiltrated from without—places where outside influences are granted entrance.

The story of the inception of this chapter about *Flow Chart* is similarly relational: My friend Robert Puccinelli showed me an excerpt of the poem published in *The Paris Review*. Immediately, I sensed that this poem behaved differently than other poems I've read. I felt it pull me in and then push me away. I needed to read more of it. It demanded to be read aloud and with others. Although what I read in *The Paris Review* was a fragment of the whole—a selection taken from somewhere in the middle of the poem—it made sense on its own (as much as one could say any passage of *Flow Chart* makes sense). Despite being part of a book-length poem, this passage, amongst others from *Flow Chart*, functioned like a fragment: entirely self-sufficient and yet part of a greater whole. This self-sufficiency of the parts of the poem is due to their cadence. The poem repeats a rhythm throughout; it performs absoluteness through its undulations, which require the reader to be set into motion, and which can be felt, even when they do not mean.

The poem was composed in the span of time between the death of Ashbery's mother and Ashbery's sixtieth birthday—the space between death and birth—but it is not about his mother, nor is it about Ashbery himself. And, in spite of its repeated use of the first-person pronoun and the fact that it feels as if our narrator is telling us about his own life, the poem is not an autobiography of anyone in particular.[3] The "I" could refer to the poet himself or a character in the scene. The "you" could include or exclude the reader; or, it might be an address from the poet to himself.[4] Proper names are either popular, generic, or fictional.[5]

In the following passages from *Flow Chart*—indicative of the type of writing one is prone to find in its over 200 extra wide pages—Ashbery's stream-like style is apparent. Speaking in the first person (although the reader cannot assume that the first person is actually Ashbery himself), the poem's speaker tells someone that under his "austere façade," he is really a "pussycat" and then quickly says, perhaps addressing the reader, "Speaking of cats, when was the last time you spoke to one, calling it by its name?" The speaker continues on to discuss loneliness, the nature of life, and the end of his life. Death—a theme that is repeated frequently throughout *Flow Chart*—provides it with some continuity. Without any warning, Ashbery's speaker briefly turns his attention to the topic of pudding ("Sprinkled with coconut, perhaps?") before moving on to discussing the evening when "you get down to business" and pretzel sticks. The section breaks off there "for the reason things do get broken off: it's amusing. Love, The Human Pool Table."[6] In another passage where Ashbery seems to be writing about his own writing process or the writing process in general, the speaker mentions that he is looking for a pen and asks for someone to cancel all of his appointments; then, he switches topics to watering a houseplant, curling the hair of his addressee, an upstate visitor, and how the bush has grown.[7] Like many others in *Flow Chart*, this section keeps charging forward without thematic focus. The reader of *Flow Chart* is unable to take away a specific message, story, or narrative. It is difficult to provide a summary of what *Flow Chart* is about, because it is not about anything or anyone in particular.

Reading Ashbery's *Flow Chart* would be undoubtedly frustrating for a reader bent on comprehending the poem's meaning. There is no obvious order or pattern to the text. There is no clear subject in either sense of the word. There are no repeating characters. The experience of reading the poem can, however, be conceived in terms of its rhythm.[8] The poem contains movements and counter-movements. It feels as though the shape of a distinct wave comes into view; the reader begins to conjure up an image in her mind; and, just as quickly, the image crashes onto the shore and dissolves into foam. At moments in *Flow Chart*, a scene with characters begins to come into focus and, just as swiftly, the resolution becomes fuzzy, faded, and the image is entirely out of view. Non sequitur. We are on to a new topic altogether. This method of storytelling is akin to finding ephemeral pictures in the clouds and it is, I will argue, a method of enacting the same poetic mysticism as Schlegel's fragmentary writings.

THE INTERPRETATIONS

Interpretations of *Flow Chart*, like the text itself, offer the reader a range of possibilities. The poem has been described as a metaphor for life, as surrealist landscape painting, as autobiography, and as the making of music even when it doesn't make sense.[9] Stephen Koch describes Ashbery's "poetic voice" as a "hushed, simultaneously incomprehensible and intelligent whisper with a weird pulsating rhythm that fluctuates like a wave between peaks of sharp clarity and watery troughs of obscurity and languor."[10] Through its wave-like movement, the poem challenges the reader's attempts at creating a narrative. The poem resists the reader's desire for closure, her impulse to define and fix its meaning, or to "figure it out." At every turn, or turn of phrase, it rejects the picture that the reader creates in her mind. It takes away, only to give again.

In *Flow Chart*'s opening lines, the poem's speaker recalls reading a poem, but he says that he had forgotten what he was reading or how it was supposed to make him feel. These early lines are perhaps a gesture, on Ashbery's part, to prepare his audience for the experience of reading this poem. With *Flow Chart*, forgetfulness is not merely incidental. It is nearly impossible to remember what the poem is about. *Flow Chart* is devoid of tangible specifics held together by a story; it lacks those elements that would produce the friction necessary to offer the reader something to hold onto, a bit of meaning that she could later recollect. *Flow Chart* is not the outward expression of the artist's inner landscape;

it does not contain the reflections of an individual at all. Rather, the poem speaks from within a group, but we do not know what group. It describes actions being taken by actors and things being said, but we have no idea why, or to whom. Bonnie Costello describes Ashbery's poems through the comparison with surrealist landscape painters. A landscape is defined as what can be captured in one glance; in this respect, the landscape operates as a metaphor for knowledge, i.e., as the frame for knowledge.[11] Ashbery creates landscapes with words; however, on Costello's analysis, his landscapes are surrealistic frames for knowledge; each of Ashbery's shifting landscapes captures a place that could exist anywhere or nowhere.

The poem's title is also an indication of its structure and method. A flow chart is a visual diagram that provides a linear order and organization to ideas. With this definition in mind, the poem could be interpreted as a general outline of some kind of narrative, merely offering the rubric within which the flow would happen. Ashbery supports this reading when he describes his own work as a "generalized transcript."[12] But what is the poem transcribing? Whose story is it telling? If it is an autobiography, then it is "anybody's autobiography."[13] However, it does not follow from the claim that the poem is "anybody's autobiography" that it refers to a universal knower, i.e., a featureless abstraction that would function as a stand-in for anyone anywhere. Rather, *Flow Chart* refers to a general time and place; as is suggested by the title, this time and place could be the corporate and institutional post-Reagan world in which the poem was composed.[14]

As a metaphor for life, a flow chart combines "the spontaneous passage of living matter" with "its organized selective record."[15] However, *Flow Chart*, as life, is not merely a general outline or transcript, which would precede the events it charts, and which could subsist separate from them. Rather, *Flow Chart* exhibits what Schlegel calls coarse irony, i.e., the unity of opposites that courses through the nature of things: It "has lucid moments and long passages of inexplicable, disconnected activity; like life too, it is alternately exciting and boring, mysterious and obvious, fascinating and tedious."[16] The events the poem presents are related through an "inexorable and interconnected pattern,"[17] which relentlessly charges forward without permitting the reader to capture its meaning.[18] The pattern or chart does not precede the flow of the poem's content, but rather emerges from out of it.

The coincidence of opposites that gives rise to the title of the poem can also be considered topographically. John Shoptaw suggests that the "flow" in *Flow Chart* can be conceived as the Hudson River that runs past both Ashbery's Manhattan and Hudson Valley homes; the chart, in this case, is the railway that follows the river's course. A river is the physical manifestation of the coincidence of opposites, or the irony that courses through this text, insofar as it promises both "a unity of origin and destination and a fluctuating Heraclitan difference."[19] As the river flows, its movements can be read by those who are fluent in deciphering its meanings. For example, a "pillow" in a river indicates a rock or obstruction; it appears as a bulge in the water that is "both stationary and fluid," because even as the water is moving and changing every second, the shape of the pillow remains constant.[20] A "pillow" is just one example of the legibility of the movements of water; for travelers in kayaks, or other small crafts, such fluency in the language of the river is crucial for avoiding dangerous, and even deadly, situations. The movements of the river can be tracked using the terms used to describe it; however, the river and its movements, or the flow and chart of Ashbery's poem, are as inextricably linked as the form and content of any artwork. In the case of *Flow Chart*, the fact that its content remains nonspecific is precisely what produces its form as a "generalized transcript." Like the manifestation of the "pillow" in the river, the form of *Flow Chart* is not a husk that precedes its content, but rather the form, i.e., the general outline or transcript, is produced through the nonspecific content of the poem. As with the river's shapes, the form of the poem is the result of the monotonous flow of its content. With this background into the poem's origins, structure, and interpretation in mind, I now turn to the four thematic points of connection with Schlegel.

INCOMPREHENSIBILITY

In "On Incomprehensibility," Schlegel responds to his critics who misunderstood the *Athenaeum* fragments. However, rather than clarifying the meaning of those fragments and therefore resolving the misunderstanding, he declares that the incomprehensibility of the *Athenaeum* fragments is due to the irony that is found everywhere in them. Any attempt to clarify the irony of the fragments would make them unironic and thereby destroy the very method by which it is possible to approach the Absolute. That is, in the process of attempting to fully comprehend the ironic fragments, the knower would destroy the very quality of the fragments that allows them to perform absoluteness. The desire for complete comprehension destroys the possibility of comprehending the whole. The unbridled activity of the understanding destroys its object in the process of trying to know it. Thus, restraint is necessary in order to intuit the whole. In order to accomplish this latter task, philosophical writing must not only remain ironic, but also fragmentary; to turn the fragments into a completed system, or to fill in the (literal and figurative) gaps between them, would also destroy their capacity for realizing the whole.

Schlegel urges his readers to cultivate versatility of mind instead of attempting to comprehend the world. In *Athenaeum* fragment 121, Schlegel emphasizes the role of the imagination when he describes what it means to have a versatile mind. Versatility entails being able to "transport oneself arbitrarily now into this, now into that sphere as if into another world, not merely with one's reason [*Verstand*] and imagination [*Einbildung*], but with one's whole soul [*Seele*]; to freely relinquish first one and then another part of one's being, and confine oneself entirely to a third."[21] In this fragment, Schlegel invokes the imagination; however, the imagination is not being appealed to as the motor for the creative activity of an unchecked ego. Rather, it is the means for fully inhabiting other worlds, and, in the process, for placing a limit on the ego that thinks it can comprehend the whole. In its capacity of transporting us to different worlds, the imagination serves as a check on the ego, because it shows us that all perspectives are partial (or put differently, all perspectives are wholly true but only from within themselves). In "Irony and Romantic Subjectivity," Fred Rush points out that in general art allows the viewer to inhabit many different viewpoints, and ironic art does this even more so.[22] It is precisely irony that cultivates the agility of mind to inhabit different worlds, views, and interpretations.

Ashbery's text continually transports its reader; she is shuttled between different places, people, times, and themes. *Flow Chart* vacillates between moments of poignant truth and clarity, which, as quickly as they arise, turn into moments of utter incomprehensibility. Ashbery might begin a section with an ostensibly clear statement ("Words, however are not the culprit. They are at worst a placebo"), and then end the same passage with a statement of seeming nonsense ("It's better though to listen to the strange chirps of furniture").[23] The reader is so frequently transported while reading *Flow Chart* that she is never on firm footing; instead, she can only follow the rhythm of the text or, better yet, persevere through its more than 200 pages. John Emil Vincent argues that perseverance is also evident in the way the text is written; it is a text that is not the result of poetic energy, but of a "persistence against lethargy."[24]

Like the *Dao De Jing*, Schlegel's fragments and Ashbery's *Flow Chart* are texts that are marked by their emptiness. The emptiness of these texts is the source of their incomprehensibility. In the image of the clay pot from the *Dao De Jing*, the empty center of the pot cannot be grasped, but it is necessary in order for the pot to perform its function of containing. At the meta-textual level, the *Dao De Jing* also contains spaces—it is a cryptic poem consisting of paradoxes and riddles that are never resolved. The text cannot be assimilated by its reader's understanding because, like the clay pot, indeterminacy is part of its structure. Likewise, Schlegel's ironic fragments point us to their incompleteness and to the gaps within and between them. *Flow Chart* remains general and does not fill in all the gaps for the reader's understanding. It is precisely because Schlegel's fragments and Ashbery's poem are not entirely comprehensible that they are able to bring the reader in contact with the Absolute. What initially appears as a lack is indeed essential to their method from performing absoluteness. Paradoxically, by not totalizing, they get closer to what is total. To really get at the whole, our method for communicating must also contain within itself the space or opening of incomprehensibility. And, as a result of their incomprehensibility, these texts are open to new interpretations by future readers, as well as the possibility of being misunderstood.

SYSTEMATICITY

If broken apart into its components parts, the title of Ashbery's poem, *Flow Chart*, expresses Schlegel's pronouncement in *Athenaeum* fragment 53 that the mind ought to combine both having and not having a system.[25] The "flow" of *Flow Chart* indicates the way in which the poem is written in a stream-like style. It flows, again, like waves; sentences run together and then break apart; topics of conversation blur; at one moment the poem's speaker is talking about cats, then the nature of death, suddenly pudding. The "chart," or the systematicity of *Flow Chart*, is introduced, in part, by the reader of the poem who continually struggles to grasp at a narrative structure of some kind in terms of a theme, a central idea, or perhaps a recurring character. The reader brings a desire for structure and coherence to the poem, but this desire is never fully satisfied. However, these moments when a narrative begins to crystalize are not a mere figment of the reader's imagination either; certain clauses do repeat ideas (e.g., about cats, pretzels, life, and death). The poem lends itself to patterns, which the reader's mind attempts to synthesize into a holistic picture; however, just as quickly as the poem provides the basis for a coherent narrative, it breaks apart any possible narrative structure by moving on to another, unconnected (or apparently disconnected) idea or stream of thought. Like the Hudson River it was compared to earlier, the poem slips through the reader's fingers; it is ungraspable. In its movements, the poem resists its reader's impulse to determine its meaning.

The poem's resistance to closure is not only presented through its movement, but also in the content of its lines. *Flow Chart* begins with a reference to a diagram and ends with the line: "It's open: the bridge, that way."[26] In both its first and last lines, it gestures toward its own incompleteness. A diagram (one example being, of course, the flow chart) is a simplified representation or a schematic; like the idea of a "generalized transcript," it does not include a level of detail that would fix and determine its meaning and application. A bridge is a concrete structure, but one that signifies openness—a path, that way. The poem does not tell us what is "that way." It merely ends by pointing off the page, into empty space.

In Schlegel's philosophical project, the mind's decision to combine having a system with not having a system is reflected in the form of his writings: the ironic fragments. The fragments are not entirely unsystematic; they contain proper syntax and grammar; they are numbered; the fragments can be read together, and, in their union, they illuminate each other. However, there is no combination of the fragments that would yield a completed system; there is no fragment that provides the foundational principle or the conclusion to the system of fragments. Moreover, insofar as the fragments are ironic, another degree of openness is introduced through their content: Their meaning is not fixed and may multiply. In other words, for Schlegel, it is not merely the mind that decides whether it will complete the system, but irony that shows us that the task of completing the system is impossible. The text itself, through its irony, resists our attempts at closure. However, this interruption (or gap) is a necessary part of the whole that cannot be recuperated, but which must be indirectly communicated if what we seek is the Absolute. The fragment regarding the mind's relationship to systems is not merely a command about what the mind ought to do, but it is also a performance of that imperative; that is, as ironic, it demands the joining of two opposites: the systematic and the unsystematic. As a fragment, it is self-standing but also a part of the collection of the fragments; together the fragments create a network of meanings, but one that is incomplete and never to be completed.

GENIUS

The role of incomprehensibility in both Schlegel and Ashbery's texts marks a shift away from the conception of genius as a sovereign master who is in complete control over the resulting work. Recall that, in *The Laboratory of Poetry*, Michel Chaouli argues that the fragments are laboratories in which experiments of joining and mixing take place. Some words—or elements of words—have affinities toward one another; they are attracted to one another. Others do not. Two consequences of this experimental model are of note for the present analysis: 1) an increase in the sheer number of possible combinations, some of which are nonsensical or unheard-of; 2) art becomes more autonomous and art's autonomy is measured by the number of novel, sometimes incomprehensible, combinations that arise. As art becomes more autonomous, incomprehensible combinations will arise with higher frequency.[27]

This shift in genius is tied to Schlegel's transformation of the meaning of irony. In the rhetorical meaning of irony, i.e., to say one thing but mean another, the ironic utterance relies upon an agreement between the listener and speaker in which both understand that the speaker intends something other than what she says. The "true" meaning of the statement is conveyed in some predictable way, for example, through the speaker's tone or through the statement's context. Irony, in this model, is just one rhetorical device that the author uses to achieve her ultimate aim. With Schlegel's transformation of irony, the writer now says two things at once, contradictory but equally true. The writer may fail to convey this at all, or the reader may only pick up on the meaning of the statement in part. In the ironic utterance, a second meaning is revealed, but the author is not always in control and can never be fully in control. Once the text breaks open to reveal an additional meaning, this opening cannot be contained. The writer risks being outwitted by the words, whose relationships with each other exceed the role of human agency. In Schlegel's experimental fragment-laboratories, the genius can no longer be conceived of in terms of the sovereign-master over the words on the page, even at the moments where she *seems* to have lost control. Under this experimental model, the author (as genius) is no longer in complete control, but rather her genius is exhibited by her willingness to risk the incomprehensibility that occurs in these experiments of joining and mixing of the elements, i.e., the words or word parts. An intimacy with irony acquaints her with the way in which the meaning of words can double and how they can outwit even the cleverest philosopher.[28] The writer under this new model of genius is humble before the words, rather than the master of them. Similarly, in his "Monologue," Novalis claims that language is self-sufficient and only concerned with itself. He states that if an individual aims to say something definite and fixed, then she says the "most ridiculous false stuff." On the other hand, when she speaks just for the sake of speaking—when she babbles—the "most splendid, original truths" emerge.[29] Toward the end of this very short "monologue," Novalis catches himself: He is, indeed, declaring something definite and specific about the nature of language. Is he erring in doing so? In this moment of self-reflection, Novalis posits that the writer's vocation is marked by being inspired by language—by being called to write by a force greater than herself.

The comportment of the writer who yields to the words can be illustrated through the Daoist images of water. Water is an image for the power that arises from passivity, from relinquishing control. The comparison with water evokes an image of the writer as the one who yields and who flows; this is a stark contrast to the analytic writer's preoccupation with mastery and control, i.e., of fixing the meaning of the words and their effect on her audience. To be like water is to master non-mastery, but this is no easy task. With language, the mastery of non-mastery requires that the writer be intimate with words and humble before their relationships with each other; it is a return to the innocence at the beginning—a second innocence—by way of a path cleared of the "thickets of clichés."[30]

Ashbery's *Flow Chart* is the product of an author who is willing to subject his writing to the forces beyond his control. The work's autonomy, measured by its incomprehensibility, is due, in part, to Ashbery's writing process. One element of Ashbery's writing process that lends to the production of an autonomous work is his use of "managed chance."[31] Like the title, *Flow Chart*, the phrase "managed chance" is also an apparent contradiction. "Managed chance" refers to the introduction of chance into the writing process, but in a way pre-determined by the author. For example, Ashbery keeps the telephone on and answers calls while he is writing.[32] Words and phrases from his phone conversations then enter into the poem. Ashbery cannot predict who will be on the line or what they may say; however, he remains in control of the element of chance insofar as he has chosen to leave the phone on. As the poet of a "generalized transcript," Ashbery transmits what comes through the phone.

Similar to the intervention of the telephone, in Ashbery's Chelsea home, all the drawers, cabinets, and closet doors are open, allowing for all possibilities. Ashbery reads portions of poems from other authors and then puts them down abruptly, not allowing all of a poet's influence to enter into his work, but also not entirely excluding the influence of the people and objects that surround him.[33] In a 2005 profile on Ashbery in *The New Yorker*, Larissa MacFarquhar, observes Ashbery's behavior before he finally sits down at the typewriter. She notes,

> He picks up his cup of tea and takes two small sips because it's still quite hot. He puts it down. He's supposed to write some poetry today. . . . He had some coffee. He read the newspaper. He dipped into a couple of books: a Proust biography that he bought five years ago but just started reading because it suddenly occurred to him to do so, a novel by Jean Rhys that he recently came across in a second-

hand bookstore—he's not a systematic reader. He flipped on the television and watched half of something dumb.[34]

After reading this description of Ashbery's process, we might be inclined to say that any writer has similar procrastination techniques, or that everyone who writes take pauses, meanders, or flits about before beginning their work. However, what distinguishes Ashbery from other poets and writers is that he allows this "extra stuff" into his poems, or rather, he doesn't exclude it. Ashbery doesn't polish the finished product to remove outside influences and eliminate the impression of breaks in the writing process. The result is a poem with an episodic quality; it contains pauses. A friend, describing *Flow Chart*, said: "you can almost hear when he sets the pen down each day" (or, more accurately, when he leaves the typewriter). Christopher Schmidt remarks, "[one] of Ashbery's great contributions to twentieth-century American literature is his embrace of the contingent and the accidental; accordingly, Ashbery's revision process is unusually light."[35] The reader senses that there was little effort to make the poem *about something*, to give it a holistic quality, or to provide it with some determinate meaning that the reader could take away from it. Ashbery does not smooth out the edges for us—he does not try to create a work that is free of outside influences and that thereby reflects the mind of a solitary creator.

Like the drawers and cabinets in Ashbery's Chelsea home, the poem is open to its reader. This reader will make certain decisions, draw some conclusions and not others. When reading this massive poem printed on extra-wide pages, the reader will make choices about where to pause as she becomes out of breath (or, more often, her lung capacity will make this choice for her). She will undoubtedly be forced to put this tome down and pick it up later. While Ashbery's poem does include section breaks, they are merely resting points, and do not impose a break in a narrative line like a book chapter might.

The misrepresentative poetics of Ashbery's texts introduces an additional potential incomprehensibility at the level of the language of the poem. A text is misrepresentative insofar as there are words and themes that do not appear at all, but which are also not consciously excluded. In *On the Outside Looking Out*, John Shoptaw refers to the words that are left out of the poem and only pointed to in their absence "crypt words." Crypt words are not concealed, rather they are "on the outside looking out"; they do not appear in the poem at all. And, it is through their not appearing that their power is released.[36] Shoptaw discusses an aspect of Ashbery's poetry, which Ashbery himself leaves out: his sexuality. Because Ashbery leaves his homosexuality out of his poems, they behave in ways that Shoptaw terms "homotextual," i.e., the poems behave differently despite their subject matter.[37] This misrepresentation was not only a poetic strategy, but also a survival one in the era of McCarthyism during which Ashbery's poetics evolved.[38] Shoptaw cites Ashbery's *The Vermont Notebook* (1975) as another example of misrepresentative poetics. This hybrid text, which includes drawings provided by Ashbery's artist friend Joe Brainard, misrepresents insofar it is titled *The Vermont Notebook*, but it was largely written on busses in New England outside of Vermont. At the same time, Ashbery might protest and say that the text does not actually misrepresent, insofar as the content of the poem could refer to Vermont just as well as New Hampshire. That is, Ashbery is writing a "generalized transcript" that could have taken place on a bus ride in Vermont, or some other locale. However, to say that the poem could refer to Vermont just as well as another location is not a claim to universality; rather, Ashbery is an American writer and a prosaic one, and his poetry reflects a general sense of time and place.

In 1957, Ashbery wrote a review of Gertrude Stein's *Stanzas in Meditation* for *Poetry* magazine. Ashbery's review of Stein's poem reads as an uncanny description of his own poem, *Flow Chart*, which he will publish more than thirty years later. Describing Stein's poem, he writes that it "gives one the feeling of time passing, of things happening, of a 'plot,' though it would be difficult to say precisely what is going on."[39] Addressing the worry of critics about the poem's potential monotony, he writes, "[there] is certainly plenty of monotony in the 150-page title poem which forms the first half of this volume, but it is the fertile kind, which generates excitement as water monotonously flowing over a dam generates electrical power."[40] This description of the poem's monotony connects to the preceding analysis a number of ways. First, this critique of Stein's poem is another example of Ashbery's misrepresentative poetics. Christopher Schmidt points out that Ashbery's description creates a "dream dam" through a metaphor, which is "slyly convincing and totally unreal," since "dammed water passes *through* turbines housed within the dam or adjacent to it, not *over* the dam, as Ashbery suggests."[41] Like Stein, Ashbery creates a "counterfeit of reality more real than reality" through his misrepresentative poetics.[42]

Second, Ashbery's description of the dam resonates with the descriptions of water as an expression of dark efficacy in the *Dao De Jing*. Water is often conceived as soft and weak, but because it has no shape of its own, it can take on any shape. Because water has no agency of its own, it merely flows to the lowest place, thereby stimulating the fertility of the valley. And, although monotonous, the flow of water is quite powerful. The image of water flowing over the dam illustrates dark efficacy as a source of power that is counterintuitive to the prototypical conception of power. In other words, what is conventionally viewed as weak can be great. Although, like the description of water, *Flow Chart* is often bland or monotonous, the poem's movements, like dammed water, generate great power. The monotonous flow of content produces a form that is great, because it facilitates an intuition of the whole. Dark efficacy is also connected to the *yin* aspect of Nature, i.e., the crucial role of passivity and receptivity for the harmonious flow of the whole. With regard to the *yin* aspect, Ashbery's writing style has a porous quality; it allows outside influences to penetrate it. Additionally, in the *Dao De Jing*, water is a metaphor for both the *Dao* and the ruler insofar as it cannot be grasped. The ruler is devoid of any mastery or know-how that would make him susceptible to being mastered by anyone and the *Dao* is no-thing and therefore cannot be grasped or comprehended. Similarly, *Flow Chart*'s nonspecific content cannot be easily grasped by its reader's understanding.

The efficacy of Ashbery's poems, or their "poetic strength," is the result of those extraneous elements that artists generally discard in order to produce a final, finished product. Dark efficacy is at work in Ashbery's poem through the inclusion of "extra material," such as the "fertile kind" of monotony. Christopher Schmidt argues that *The Vermont Notebook* establishes a "queer nature" by recognizing that waste (e.g., the landfill or dump) has the "power to disrupt the tidy categories that govern and normalize our behavior," notably the categories of nature and culture.[43] At the level of the text, waste also disrupts the "boundaries of poetic propriety."[44] Ashbery's poetic strength, Schmidt argues further, is a result of his recuperation of what is normally deemed aesthetic waste: monotonous writing, lists and logs of what he passes in the bus, the scatological, and recycled pieces of his own poems. Schmidt claims further that Ashbery's poetic genius lies in the incorporation of what other artists deemed extraneous, or those "fragments typically chiseled away from the work."[45] Ashbery echoes this claim when he describes his own writing as free association that includes "all kinds of extra material that doesn't belong—but does."[46] But what does it mean for that "extra material" to belong and simultaneously not belong? This statement, like the ironic fragments, is self-contradictory; it illuminates, while obscuring, its own meaning. Its meaning can be intuited—in a flash of insight—but when unpacked into discrete statements, it begins to fall apart.

Given the role of contingency and the infiltration of outside influences, how does Ashbery's poetry retain any coherence? One possible site for coherence is that it all comes from the poet Ashbery.[47] But the sense of the poet as the sovereign and solitary artist is already disrupted by the use of managed chance, by the intervention of the caller on the line, by the open drawers, cabinets, and books, by words that misrepresent or do not appear at all, and by waste in its various meanings. These elements contribute to the poem's autonomy, as its independence from its creator; and, with this independence, the possibility for incomprehensible utterances increases.

THE READER

The early German romantics were not only a group of philosophers and artists, but a close-knit group of friends. Whether it is the relationship with one's peers or the inner relationship with one's self, *symphilosophie* or *sympoetry* is a sacred friendship. The synthetic writer cultivates this philosophical friendship by approaching her reader as "alive and critical." Each of these terms—synthetic and *symphilosophie*—contain prefixes that mean "with" or "together," thereby underscoring the fact that the synthetic writer is the one who is engaged in *symphilosophie*. In contrast with the analytic writer, the synthetic writer does not attempt to make a particular impression upon her reader but rather "enters with him into the sacred [*heilige*] relationship of deepest symphilosophy or sympoetry."[48] The author-reader relationship is a holy [*heilige*] one concerned with the lofty task of approaching the Absolute. It is a sacred communion between the author and her reader in which the two pursue an intuition of the whole.

Both Schlegel and Ashbery are synthetic writers engaged in the project of *symphilosophie* or *sympoetry*. Their texts do not merely aim to make the appropriate impression upon their reader; moreover, these texts need the reader in order to perform absoluteness. The ironic fragments are not easily comprehended, they require the time, patience, and energy of a reader who is willing to persevere, even as, like the hedgehog, they curl into a ball and evade our understanding. Likewise, Ashbery's poem requires the persistence of the reader whose engagement is required to set the poem's movements into motion and to allow those movements to continue.

Through her enduring engagement with these texts, the reader cultivates a mind that is agile or versatile. In Schlegel's fragments, agility is the result of the repeated exposure to irony. Ironic texts avoid the fixity and one-sidedness of other philosophical approaches by tempting the reader to consider contradictory claims in one concise statement. With regard to the text's meaning, irony is a source of its fertility and depth; however, irony carries the risk that the reader will misunderstand the text, i.e., that she will approach the text as fixed or one-sided by only taking one of its meanings to be the case. Agility is a precondition for sensing the irony of a text and for avoiding the misunderstandings produced by a mind that wishes merely to resolve a contradiction and thus reduce the text's meaning. The condition of agility poses a dilemma for the ironic writer, since, to approach a text as ironic (or even potentially ironic) requires the agility of mind that irony cultivates in its reader. This means that the reader of the ironic text is always a reader in delay or a reader that must be trained by the very text she wishes to understand. Moreover, there is no guarantee that the text will succeed in producing a reader who can decipher its meaning.

For Ashbery, agility is produced through the text's wave-like movement, which offers its reader moments of lucid storytelling and then quickly sweeps those away—only to repeat this process. The feeling of reading *Flow Chart* is like having a rug constantly tugged underneath one's feet. As with the ironic fragments, agility or versatility of mind enables the reader to engage with the poem (as opposed to setting it down in frustration), but this agility is precisely what the poem cultivates in its reader. *Flow Chart* produces a reader with a mind that resembles the flow chart, which can shuttle back and forth between contradictory ideas without attempting to close the system, to "figure it out," or to have the last word. An agile mind does not seek full mastery, but instead it is able to sense the spaces or gaps where what is unknown dwells among the known. In this relationship of *sympoetry*, the synthetic writer cannot depend on an already existing reader who is prepared to understand him and the risk of misunderstanding looms. In the case of *Flow Chart*, a possible source of misunderstanding could be the assumption that the poem is meant to be understood in the first place.

CONCLUSION

Following a playful iteration of the common children's saying—I'm rubber, you're glue—Ashbery writes, "in which gluey / embrace I surrender / We are both part of a living thing now."[49] The "living thing" that we are part of when we read Ashbery's poem is the Absolute. The Absolute as absolute is non-relational; this means that separating the knower from the Absolute would introduce a relationship and thereby limit the Absolute. The Absolute includes the poet-reader-knower. By bringing us into its "gluey embrace," *Flow Chart* is a poem in the rare sense described in the opening to this chapter: The poem performs absoluteness and offers its reader an intuition of the whole. However, it cannot do this on its own; the poem requires the reader's breath, attention, and imagination to bring its sacred undulations to life.

Flow Chart is a poem that offers the reader an intuition of a dynamic Absolute. The poem's wave-like movement is set into motion when the reader tries to grasp at the poem's meaning or when she conjures up images for its content; these images that she produces soon disappear as the poem swiftly moves on to another disconnected topic. In its relationship with the text, the reader's mind oscillates between moments of clear structure and narrative to sheer nonsense. The reader is constantly transported from one landscape to another, all of which are lacking a central storyline, character, or even theme. It is, as I said earlier, like trying to read pictures in the clouds, which dissipate almost as quickly as they are formed. It is impossible to grasp or determine the poem's meaning, but it is not entirely meaningless either. The poem alternates between lucid and nonsensical statements in a way that keeps its meaning open-ended. Through its movement, the poem makes possible an intuition of the movement of the Absolute for the reader who is ready to be its willing participant.

Schlegel's and Ashbery's texts rely on their reader to incite their movement and are thus not entirely self-sufficient. Likewise, the intuition of the whole, on the part of the reader, depends on a text, which that intuition is tethered to and traceable back to. These authors are in a sacred communion of *symphilosophie* or *sympoetry* with their readers; their task is the highest one: an intuition of the Absolute. Schlegel advises the readers of the fragments that they "shouldn't try to symphilosophize with everyone, but only with those who are *à la hauteur*."[50] The text requires the energetic effort of those who are willing to enter into a relationship with it, rather than merely consume it. At the same time, it resists our desire to easily digest its meaning, and thus cultivates this very relationship of non-mastery that is a pre-condition for the intuition of the whole.

This intuition of the whole through the experience of reading the text is what I am calling "poetic mysticism" in Schlegel, Ashbery, and the *Dao De Jing*. Poetic mysticism is tied to a particular text, which skillfully uses language against its propensity to grasp and thereby cultivates a mind in its readers that is agile enough to realize the whole. The relationship produced between the text and each of its readers—through the act of reading itself—is not reproducible. Because the process incorporates incomprehensibility, it is not completely rational or calculable. There is no guarantee of success; not everyone who reads Schlegel, Ashbery, or the *Dao De Jing* will have an experience of the whole. However, this is not mysticism as an intellectual intuition of the whole that is not demonstrable at all. The reader's experience of the whole—through the development of an agile or versatile mind that is able to hold two contradictory statements at once—is tethered to a text that produces, develops, and cultivates this agility in its reader. And furthermore, the text can be analyzed and its techniques for developing the reader's agility of mind and for resisting the reader's attempts to fully comprehend it can be elaborated. The techniques used by Ashbery to achieve this experience of the whole include irony as the coincidence of opposites (e.g., in the title *Flow Chart*), "managed chance," "misepresentative poetics," and the poem's wave-like movement toward and away from crystalized moments of a narrative. However, insofar as any text's means for performing absoluteness relies on contingency or irony, it will not be possible to articulate a complete systematic and rational account of how the text achieves this end.

My claim is that certain texts utilize language against its propensity to merely grasp in order to perform absoluteness as a dynamic movement. To do this, they must also train their readers to have a mind agile enough to engage with that movement, i.e., to be able to think systematically while resisting the urge to complete the system. These texts repeatedly thwart their reader's attempts to fully comprehend them through a movement by which they give meaning and then recede from a full exhaustion of that meaning. And, through their resistance (via that space of emptiness or incomprehensibility that thwarts our efforts at mastery), they offer their readers more. Paradoxically, by resisting our attempts to fully comprehend them, these texts bring their readers into contact with the whole.

NOTES

1. Schlegel, *Lucinde and the Fragments*, 143, CF 4.
2. John Emil Vincent, *John Ashbery and You: His Later Books* (University of Georgia Press, 2007), 47–48.
3. Although I claim that the poem's speaker is not necessarily Ashbery, I will retain the masculine pronouns (he/him/his) whenever referring to or citing the poem for the sake of maintaining its fluidity.
4. Emil Vincent, *John Ashbery and You*, 52.
5. John Shoptaw, *On the Outside Looking Out: John Ashbery's Poetry* (Cambridge, MA: Harvard University Press, 1995), 304–305.
6. John Ashbery, *Flow Chart: A Poem*, 1st ed. (New York: Knopf, 1991), 170.
7. Ibid., 98.
8. Novalis refers to his *Romantic Encyclopedia* as the seed of all books. I argue elsewhere that this seed is the rhythm of the text, i.e., the repetition of the romantic coupling of the disciplines. That is, the seed is not a foundational principle, but rather the movement or musicality that permeates the work. Karolin Mirzakhan, "Romantic Irony," in *The Palgrave Handbook of German Romantic Philosophy*, edited by Elizabeth Millán Brusslan, forthcoming with Palgrave-Macmillan.
9. Fred Moramarco argues for the repetition of metaphors of life in Ashbery's writing, particularly in *Flow Chart*. Fred Moramarco, "Coming Full

Circle: John Ashbery's Later Poetry," in *The Tribe of John: Ashbery and Contemporary Poetry*, ed. Susan M. Schultz (Tuscaloosa: University Alabama Press, 1995). Bonnie Costello compares Ashbery's landscapes to surrealist painting. Bonnie Costello, "John Ashbery's Landscapes," in *The Tribe of John: Ashbery and Contemporary Poetry*, ed. Susan M. Schultz (Tuscaloosa: University Alabama Press, 1995), 60–82. In his monograph on Ashbery, Shoptaw describes *Flow Chart* as an autobiography about no one in particular. John Shoptaw, *On the Outside Looking Out: John Ashbery's Poetry* (Cambridge, MA: Harvard University Press, 1995). In a book chapter on Ashbery, Shoptaw describes Ashbery's poetry as the making of music. John Shoptaw, "The Music of Construction: Measure and Polyphony in Ashbery and Bernstein," in *The Tribe of John: Ashbery and Contemporary Poetry*, ed. Susan M. Schultz (Tuscaloosa: University Alabama Press, 1995).

10. Stephen Koch, "The New York School of Poets: The Serious at Play," *New York Times*, February 11, 1968, sec. Archives, https://www.nytimes.com/1968/02/11/archives/the-new-york-school-of-poets-the-serious-at-play.html.

11. Bonnie Costello, "John Ashbery's Landscapes," 61–63.

12. Quoted in Shoptaw, *On the Outside Looking Out*, 4.

13. Shoptaw, *On the Outside Looking Out*, 310.

14. Moramarco, "Coming Full Circle: John Ashbery's Later Poetry," 40.

15. Shoptaw, *On the Outside Looking Out*, 307.

16. Moramarco, "Coming Full Circle," 45.

17. Ibid., 40.

18. For the romantics, this organization of events great and small is the task of the novel, which, as Novalis puts it, "romanticizes" by elevating the mundane while also making the mysterious ordinary. These two inverse processes are accomplished through the pattern or constellation of events described in the novel; when every event is properly placed within the overall structure of the text, the mysterious is de-mystified and the mundane receives its proper place and significance. Romanticization is not itself an elusive or magical process, but is actualized through the labor of writing itself. HKA II, p. 545, quoted in Novalis, *Notes for a Romantic Encyclopedia: Das Allgemeine Brouillon*, ed. and trans. David W Wood (Albany: State University of New York Press, 2007), xvi.

19. Shoptaw, *On the Outside Looking Out*, 307.

20. Tristan Gooley, *How to Read Water: Clues & Patterns from Puddles to the Sea* (New York: The Experiment, 2016), 91.

21. Schlegel, *Lucinde and the Fragments*, 177. KFSA II, pp. 184–185, AF 121.

22. Fred Rush, "Irony and Romantic Subjectivity," in *Philosophical Romanticism*, ed. Nikolas Kompridis (Abingdon, OX; New York: Routledge, 2006), 182–183.

23. Ashbery, *Flow Chart*, 24–25.

24. Emil Vincent, *John Ashbery and You*, 48.

25. Schlegel, *Lucinde and the Fragments*, 167. KFSA II, p. 173, AF 53.

26. Ashbery, *Flow Chart*, 216.

27. Michel Chaouli, *The Laboratory of Poetry: Chemistry and Poetics in the Work of Friedrich Schlegel* (Baltimore: Johns Hopkins University Press, 2002), 16.

28. Judith Norman, "Hegel and Romanticism," in *Hegel and the Arts*, ed. Stephen Houlgate (Evanston, IL: Northwestern University Press, 2007), 318.

29. "Monologue," in *Classic and Romantic German Aesthetics*, ed. J. M. Bernstein (Cambridge, UK; New York: Cambridge University Press, 2003), 214–215.

30. Hélène Cixous reflects on the long journey of the writer toward a second innocence in "The Last Painting or the Portrait of God." Hélène Cixous, "The Last Painting or the Portrait of God," in *The Continental Aesthetics Reader*, ed. Clive Cazeaux, trans. Sarah Cornell (London: Routledge, 2000), 583–597.

31. Larissa MacFarquhar, "Becoming John Ashbery," October 31, 2005, https://www.newyorker.com/magazine/2005/11/07/present-waking-life.

32. Ibid.

33. Ibid.

34. Ibid.

35. Christopher Schmidt, "The Queer Nature of Waste in John Ashbery's *The Vermont Notebook*," *Arizona Quarterly: A Journal of American Literature, Culture, and Theory* 68, no. 3 (2012), 84.

36. Ibid., 8–9.

37. John Shoptaw, *On the Outside Looking Out*, 4.

38. Ibid., 4–5.

39. John Ashbery, "The Impossible: Gertrude Stein," in *Selected Prose* (University of Michigan Press, 2005), 12.

40. Ibid., 11.

41. Schmidt, "The Queer Nature of Waste in John Ashbery's *The Vermont Notebook*," 71.

42. Ashbery, "The Impossible," 15.

43. Schmidt, "The Queer Nature of Waste in John Ashbery's *The Vermont Notebook*," 72.

44. Ibid., 84.

45. Ibid., 87.

46. Quoted in Shoptaw, *On the Outside Looking Out: John Ashbery's Poetry*, 308.

47. MacFarquhar, "Becoming John Ashbery."

48. Schlegel, *Lucinde and the Fragments*, 156–157. KFSA II, p. 161, CF 112.

49. Ashbery, *Flow Chart*, 25–26.

50. Schlegel, *Lucinde and the Fragments*, 200. KFSA II, p. 210, AF 264.

BIBLIOGRAPHY

Albert, Georgia. "Understanding Irony: Three Essays on Friedrich Schlegel." *MLN* 108, no. 5 (1993).
Aristophanes. *Three Plays by Aristophanes: Staging Women*. Edited and translated by Jeffrey Henderson. New York: Routledge, 1996.
Ashbery, John. *Flow Chart*. New York: Knopf, 1991.
———. "The Impossible: Gertrude Stein." In *Selected Prose*. Ann Arbor: University of Michigan Press, 2005.
Behler, Ernst. *German Romantic Literary Theory*. Cambridge: Cambridge University Press, 1993.
———. *Irony and the Discourse of Modernity*. Seattle: University of Washington Press, 1990.
———. "The Theory of Irony in German Romanticism." In *Romantic Irony*, edited by Frederick Garber, 43–81. *A Comparative History of Literatures in European Languages*, v. 8. Budapest: Akadémiai Kiadó, 1988.
Beiser, Frederick C. *German Idealism: The Struggle against Subjectivism, 1781–1801*. Cambridge, MA.: Harvard University Press, 2002.
———. *Hegel*. New York; London: Routledge, 2005.
———. *The Romantic Imperative: The Concept of Early German Romanticism*. Cambridge, MA: Harvard University Press, 2003.
Berlin, Isaiah. *The Roots of Romanticism*. Edited by Henry Hardy. Princeton, NJ: Princeton University Press, 1999.
Bernstein, J. M, ed. *Classic and Romantic German Aesthetics*. Cambridge, UK; New York: Cambridge University Press, 2003.
Breazeale, Daniel. *Thinking Through the Wissenschaftslehre: Themes from Fichte's Early Philosophy*. New York: Oxford University Press, 2013.
Chaouli, Michel. *The Laboratory of Poetry: Chemistry and Poetics in the Work of Friedrich Schlegel*. Baltimore: Johns Hopkins University Press, 2002.
Ciardi, John. *How Does a Poem Mean?* Boston: Houghton Mifflin, 1960.
Cixous, Hélène. "The Last Painting or the Portrait of God." In *The Continental Aesthetics Reader*, edited by Clive Cazeaux, translated by Sarah Cornell, 583–597. London: Routledge, 2000.
Costello, Bonnie. "John Ashbery's Landscapes." In *The Tribe of John: Ashbery and Contemporary Poetry*, edited by Susan M. Schultz, 60–82. Tuscaloosa: University Alabama Press, 1995.
de Man, Paul. *Aesthetic Ideology*. Edited by Andrzej Warminski. Minneapolis: University of Minnesota Press, 1996.

Donougho, Martin. "Art and History: Hegel on the End, the Beginning, and the Future of Art." In *Hegel and the Arts*, edited by Stephen Houlgate, 179–215. Evanston, IL: Northwestern University Press, 2007.
Frank, Manfred. *The Philosophical Foundations of Early German Romanticism*. Translated by Elizabeth Millán-Zaibert. Albany: State University of New York Press, 2004.
Frischmann, Bärbel. "Friedrich Schlegel's Transformation of Fichte's Transcendental into an Early Romantic Idealism." In *Fichte, German Idealism, and Early Romanticism*, edited by Daniel Breazeale and Tom Rockmore. Amsterdam: Rodopi, 2010.
Gadamer, Hans Georg. *Truth and Method*. Translated by Joel Weinsheimer and Donald G. Marshall. New York: Seabury Press, 1975.
Gooley, Tristan. *How to Read Water: Clues & Patterns from Puddles to the Sea*. New York: The Experiment LLC, 2016.
Hegel, Georg Wilhelm Friedrich. *Aesthetics: Lectures on Fine Art*. Translated by T. M. Knox. 2 vols. Oxford: Clarendon Press, 1975.
———. *Faith and Knowledge*. Translated by Walter Cerf and H. S. Harris. Albany: State University of New York Press, 1977.
———. *Lectures on the Philosophy of Art: The Hotho Transcript of the 1823 Berlin Lectures*. Edited by Annemarie Gethmann-Siefert. Translated by Robert F. Brown. New York: Oxford University Press, 2014.
———. *The Difference Between Fichte's and Schelling's System of Philosophy*. Translated by H. S. Harris and Walter Cerf. Albany, NY: State University of New York Press, 1977.
———. *Werke in 20 Bänden*. 1. Aufl. Frankfurt am Main: Suhrkamp, 1986.
Houlgate, Stephen, ed. *Hegel and the Arts*. Evanston, IL.: Northwestern University Press, 2007.
———. "Hegel on the Beauty of Sculpture." In *Hegel and the Arts*, edited by Stephen Houlgate, 56–89. Evanston, IL: Northwestern University Press, 2007.
———. "Hegel's Theory of Tragedy." In *Hegel and the Arts*, edited by Houlgate, Stephen, 146–178. Evanston, IL: Northwestern University Press, 2007.
———. "Introduction: An Overview of Hegel's Aesthetics." In *Hegel and the Arts*, xi–xxviii. Evanston, IL: Northwestern University Press, 2007.
Koch, Stephen. "The New York School of Poets: The Serious at Play." *New York Times*, February 11, 1968, sec. Archives. https://www.nytimes.com/1968/02/11/archives/the-new-york-school-of-poets-the-serious-at-play.html.
Kolb, Jocelyne. "Romantic Irony." In *A Companion to European Romanticism*, edited by Michael Ferber, 376–392. Blackwell Companions to Literature and Culture. Malden, MA: Blackwell Publishers, 2005.
Lacoue-Labarthe, Philippe, and Jean-Luc Nancy. *The Literary Absolute: The Theory of Literature in German Romanticism*. Translated by Philip Barnard and Cheryl Lester. Albany: State University of New York Press, 1988.
Larmore, Charles E. *The Romantic Legacy*. New York: Columbia University Press, 1996.
Law, Stephen C. "Hegel and the Spirit of Comedy: Der Geist Der Stets Verneint." In *Hegel and Aesthetics*, edited by William Maker, 113–130. Albany: State University of New York Press, 2000.
MacFarquhar, Larissa. "Becoming John Ashbery," October 31, 2005. www.newyorker.com/magazine/2005/11/07/present-waking-life.
McCort, Dennis. "Jena Romanticism and Zen." *Discourse* 27, no. 1 (2005): 98–118.
Meillassoux, Quentin. *After Finitude: An Essay on the Necessity of Contingency*. London: Continuum Publishing, 2009.
Millán-Zaibert, Elizabeth. *Friedrich Schlegel and the Emergence of Romantic Philosophy*. Albany: State University of New York Press, 2007.
Miller, Brenda, and Suzanne Paola. *Tell It Slant: Writing and Shaping Creative Nonfiction*. Boston: McGraw-Hill Humanities, 2003.
Miller, Eric. "Masks of Negation: Greek Eironeia and Schlegel's Ironie." *ERR European Romantic Review* 8, no. 4 (1997): 360–385.
Moeller, Hans-Georg, trans. *Daodejing (Laozi): A Complete Translation and Commentary*. Chicago and La Salle, IL: Open Court, 2007.

BIBLIOGRAPHY

———. *Daoism Explained: From the Dream of the Butterfly to the Fishnet Allegory.* Open Court, 2011.
———. *The Philosophy of the Daodejing.* Columbia University Press, 2006.
Moore, A. W. *The Infinite.* Routledge, 1990.
Moramarco, Fred. "Coming Full Circle: John Ashbery's Later Poetry." In *The Tribe of John: Ashbery and Contemporary Poetry*, edited by Susan M. Schultz. Tuscaloosa, AL: University Alabama Press, 1995.
Nassar, Dalia. *The Romantic Absolute: Being and Knowing in Early German Romantic Philosophy, 1795–1804.* London and Chicago: University of Chicago Press, 2014.
Norman, Judith. "Hegel and Romanticism." In *Hegel and the Arts*, edited by Stephen Houlgate. Evanston, IL: Northwestern University Press, 2007.
Novalis. *Notes for a Romantic Encyclopedia: Das Allgemeine Brouillon.* Translated by David W. Wood. New York: SUNY Press, 2012.
———. *Novalis: Philosophical Writings.* Translated by Margaret Mahoney Stoljar. New York: SUNY Press, 1997.
Pinkard, Terry. "Symbolic, Classical, and Romantic Art." In *Hegel and the Arts*, edited by Stephen Houlgate, 3–28. Evanston, IL: Northwestern University Press, 2007.
Plato. *Meno.* Translated by G. M. A. Grube. Second Edition. Hackett Publishing Company, 1980.
Reid, Jeffrey. *The Anti-Romantic: Hegel Against Ironic Romanticism.* London; New York: Bloomsbury Academic, 2014.
Rush, Fred. "Irony and Romantic Subjectivity." In *Philosophical Romanticism*, edited by Nikolas Kompridis, 173–195. Abingdon, OX; New York: Routledge, 2006.
Schlegel, Friedrich. *Kritische Friedrich-Schlegel-Ausgabe.* Edited by Ernst Behler, Jean Jacques Anstett, and Hans Eichner. München: F. Schöningh, 1958–.
———. *Friedrich Schlegel's Lucinde and the Fragments.* Translated by Peter Firchow. Minneapolis: University of Minnesota Press, 1971.
———. "On Incomprehensibility (1800)." In *Classic and Romantic German Aesthetics*, edited by J. M. Bernstein. Cambridge, UK; New York: Cambridge University Press, 2003.
Schmidt, Christopher. "The Queer Nature of Waste in John Ashbery's *The Vermont Notebook*." *Arizona Quarterly: A Journal of American Literature, Culture, and Theory* 68, no. 3 (2012): 71–102
Schultz, Susan M., ed. *The Tribe of John: Ashbery and Contemporary Poetry.* Tuscaloosa, AL: University Alabama Press, 1995.
Shoptaw, John. *On the Outside Looking Out: John Ashbery's Poetry.* Cambridge, MA: Harvard University Press, 1995.
———. "The Music of Construction: Measure and Polyphony in Ashbery and Bernstein." In *The Tribe of John: Ashbery and Contemporary Poetry*, edited by Susan M. Schultz. Tuscaloosa: University Alabama Press, 1995.
Simpson, David, ed. *The Origins of Modern Critical Thought: German Aesthetic and Literary Criticism from Lessing to Hegel.* Cambridge [UK]; New York: Cambridge University Press, 1988.
Solomon, Robert C. *Morality and the Good Life: An Introduction to Ethics through Classical Sources.* New York: McGraw-Hill, 1984.
Stone, Alison. "Friedrich Schlegel, Romanticism, and the Re-enchantment of Nature." *Inquiry* 48, no. 1 (February 1, 2005): 3–25.
Suzuki, Shunryu. *Zen Mind, Beginner's Mind: Informal Talks on Zen Meditation and Practice.* New York: Weatherhill Inc., 1970.
Szondi, Peter. "Friedrich Schlegel and Romantic Irony, with Some Remarks on Tieck's Comedies." In *On Textual Understanding, and Other Essays.* Minneapolis: University of Minnesota Press, 1986.
Tanke, Joseph J., and Colin McQuillan, eds. *The Bloomsbury Anthology of Aesthetics.* Bloomsbury Academic, 2012.
Vincent, John Emil. *John Ashbery and You: His Later Books.* Athens: University of Georgia Press, 2007.

Wang, Robin R. *Yinyang: The Way of Heaven and Earth in Chinese Thought and Culture*. Cambridge University Press, 2012.

Zhuangzi. *Zhuangzi: The Essential Writings with Selections from Traditional Commentaries*. Translated by Brook Ziporyn. Cambridge, MA: Hackett Publishing, 2009.

INDEX

absolute, the : access to, xiv, xv, xvi, 1, 9–10, 13–14, 18, 21, 23, 26–27, 43, 45, 53–54, 59–60, 78, 81, 87, 92, 94–95, 102, 104–106; as dynamic movement (absoluteness), xvii, 12, 23, 27–28, 54, 77, 87, 88, 103, 104–106; definitions of, xiv, xviiin12, 2, 10, 21, 87, 104; ego, xvi, 37, 38–40, 43, 52, 93; problems with naming, xiv, xv, xvii, 2, 59, 75–76. *See also* Fichte; form of paradox; intuition; irony; Johann Gottlieb; mysticism, poetic

agility, xvi, 13, 14, 18, 20, 23, 47, 70, 82, 93, 103, 105–106. *See also* versatility

Aristophanes, xviiin4, 3, 6, 41–43

Ashbery, John, xiv, 87

Athenaeum, xii, 10, 14, 49, 51, 92

beautiful art, 37–38, 40. *See also* Hegel, G. W. F; Lectures on Fine Art

Behler, Ernst, 14, 29n14

Beiser, Frederick, xviiin12, 13, 24–25, 26, 32n75

Berlin, Isaiah, 33n78

Buddhism, Zen, 13–14, 31n47

chaos, 18–20, 27, 32n61, 58n46, 59, 76–77. *See also* incomprehensibility

Chaouli, Michel, 47–48, 58n46, 96. *See also* chemistry; fragment; laboratory

chemisty, 23, 48–49, 53, 58n46, 78. *See also* fragment; laboratory; Chaouli, Michel

Cixous, Hélène, 97, 108n30

comedy, ancient Greek, xviiin4, 6, 16, 29n23, 37, 40–42, 52, 57n27. *See also* Aristophanes; Hegel, G. W. F.

comprehensible, xv, 10, 13, 18–20, 24, 47, 53, 74, 76–77, 81–82, 89, 92–93, 94, 103, 105–106. *See also* understanding, faculty of

contradiction, 5, 8–12, 23, 27, 33n78, 37, 41–42, 47, 50, 54, 57n27, 57n33, 65, 74, 76, 77, 80, 96, 98, 101, 103, 105. *See also* irony, form of paradox; noncontradiction, principle of

conversation, xiii, xvi, xvii, 26, 44–45, 46, 47, 51, 94, 98. *See also* absolute, access to the; fragment

cyclical and linear models for progress, xiii, xiv, 14, 32n68, 59–60, 66, 78, 81, 91

de Man, Paul, 6–8, 26, 29n23, 33n78, 46

Dao: as creator, 68, 72, 75, 78; ideal scenario, 62, 83n11; naming, problem of, 64–65, 67–70, 73, 76, 81; nature of Nature, 62, 67, 72, 74, 75, 78, 83n7, 101; nonspecific whole 64–65, 76, 83n12; oneness, xiv, 2, 69–72; root, metaphor of, 72, 75, 77, 78; uncarved

wood 65, 70, 74; way, the, 61, 65, 71, 72, 83n11, 83n14, 95, 97; wheel, metaphor of, 32n61, 66–68, 72–74, 78, 79–81
Dao De Jing, origins of the text, 61–63
de ("power," "efficacy"), 61, 66, 74, 76–77, 81. *See also* efficacy, dark

efficacy, dark, 66, 74–75, 76–77, 80, 82, 101. *See also* de ("power," "efficacy")
emptiness, xvii, 27, 45, 47, 54, 59–60, 64–65, 66–68, 72–74, 75, 76–78, 79, 80, 81–82, 94, 95, 106

feminine, the, 65, 69, 74, 75. *See also* Dao, creator; efficacy, dark; yin
Fichte, Johann Gottlieb, 14–15, 32n64, 37–38
Flow Chart: generalized transcript, 91–92, 95, 98, 100; interpretations of, 90–92; managed chance in, xvii, 98, 102, 105; misrepresentative poetics in, 99–100, 102, 105; monotony, 82, 92, 100–101; origins of, 88–89; rhythm of, 88, 89–90, 94, 106n8; style, 89, 94; visual diagram, 91, 95
fragment, xiii, xiv, xvii, 10–12, 36, 43, 46–51, 59–60, 61, 82, 88, 92–94, 95–96, 101, 103

Gadamer, Hans-Georg, 9
genius, xvi, 5, 35–37, 38–40, 42–45, 48, 49, 50, 51, 52, 55n5, 57n35, 80, 88, 96, 101. *See also* irony, divine

Hegel, G. W. F., xvi–xvii, xviiin4, 5, 35–43, 45, 52, 54, 55n5, 56n7, 57n33, 57n35, 80

imagination, 30n38, 35, 43, 52, 93, 95, 104
in media res ("in the midst of things"), xiii, xiv, 15, 46, 54, 60
incomprehensibility, xvii, 15–20, 27, 32n61, 49, 51, 53–54, 59–60, 73, 76–77, 92–94, 96–98, 99, 105–106. *See also* chaos; emptiness; misunderstanding
infinite, xiii, xiv, 5, 12, 15, 20, 27, 46, 60, 68

intuition, xiv, xv, xvi, xviiin12, 2, 14, 27, 45, 82, 87, 92, 101–102, 104–105. *See also* absolute, access to; mysticism, poetic
irony : coarse, 16, 91–92; divine, 5, 35–38, 40, 42–43, 45, 51, 52, 80; distance and, 5–6, 39–40, 43, 44, 45–46, 47, 53, 54, 55n5, 80; encouragement to striving, 24–26, 32n75; eironeia, 3–5, 8, 16, 39, 50; form of paradox, xvi, 1, 3, 8–10, 12–13, 16–18, 21, 26, 27, 39, 47, 50, 54, 76–77, 96, 103, 105; parabasis, 6–8, 16, 26, 29n23; of irony, 16–18; restraint, functioning as, 49–50, 54; rhetorical, 5, 6, 8–10, 16, 27, 29n15, 39, 50, 96; Socratic, 3, 4, 8, 9, 13, 16, 49, 74; system of, 16–17; in the *Zhuangzi*, 63, 71. *See also* Beiser, Frederick; de Man, Paul; Hegel, G. W. F.; irony, coarse; Irony, form of paradox; Miller, Eric

Kant, Immanuel, xviiin12, 30n38, 37–38

laboratory, 47–49, 54, 96. *See also* Chaouli, Michel; chemistry; fragment
Lacoue-Labarthe, Philippe and Nancy, Jean-Luc, 12, 25
Law, Stephen C., 41–42
Lectures on Fine Art, 35, 37–38, 40, 56n7. *See also* beautiful art; Hegel, G. W. F.

Meno, xi–xii, 3, 32n75. *See also* paradox, Meno's
Millan Brusslan, Elizabeth, xviiin6, 56n6
Miller, Elaine, 16
Miller, Eric, 3–5, 22, 50
misunderstanding, xii, xviiin4, 14–15, 18–19, 25, 35, 51, 53, 78, 92, 94, 103. *See also* incomprehensibility
Moeller, Hans-Georg, 72, 75, 79, 83n12
mysticism, poetic, xv, xvi, 27, 81–82, 89, 105. *See also* absolute, access to; intuition

Nassar, Dalia, xviiin12
non-contradiction, principle of, 10
non-mastery, 79–82, 97, 105

non-presence, 9, 20, 26–27, 60, 64–65, 67, 74, 75, 76–78, 81–82, 84n18. *See also* wu 無
Norman, Judith, 49, 108n28
Novalis, xii, xiv, 9, 25, 46–47, 51, 60, 64, 75–76, 96–97, 106n8, 107n18

On Incomprehensibility, 14–18, 19, 22, 32n61, 36, 45, 48, 53, 76, 92

paradox: and the intuition of the absolute, 8, 20, 43, 82, 94, 106; in the Dao De Jing, xvii, 55, 64, 66, 67, 76, 79, 81, 94; Meno's, xi–xii, xiv, xvi, 9, 32n75. *See also* efficacy, dark; Dao, problem of naming; irony, form of paradox
philosophizing, communal activity of, xii, xiii, xiv, 46, 51, 54, 78, 81, 103
poem, 12–13, 24, 48, 87, 104. *See also* Flow Chart
poetry, romantic, 23–26, 87. *See also* religion
presence 8–10, 20, 25–26, 47, 60, 64–65, 67, 72, 74, 75, 77–78, 82, 84n18. *See also* you 有

reader, ironic, 21, 23, 25, 80, 103
reason, faculty of, 18–20, 30n38, 33n78, 38, 53, 60, 71, 93
Reid, Jeffrey, 39
religion, 25, 60
romantic: early German, xii–xv, 33n78, 46, 75, 102; striving, xiv, xv, xvi, 1–2, 8–9, 13, 24–25, 26–27, 32n75, 47, 59, 60, 87; imperative, xvi, 24–25, 54, 78; poetry. *See* poetry, romantic
romanticize, 24, 107n18. *See also* Beiser, Frederick; Novalis

sage-ruler, 61–62, 65, 66, 68, 72, 74–75, 79–80, 81–82, 84n21, 85n45
Schmidt, Christopher, 99–101
self-restraint, xvii, 4–5, 39, 43–50, 53–54
Shoptaw, John, 92, 99–100, 106n9
Socrates, xi–xii, xviiin4, 3, 8, 9, 14, 32n75, 50. *See also* irony, Socratic

Stone, Alison, 1.44
Suzuki, Shunryu. *See* Buddhism, Zen
symphilosophie, xii, 26, 51, 55n5, 102–103, 105. *See also* sympoetry
sympoetry, 103, 105
systematicity, 13, 20, 94, 95, 103, 106. *See also* fragment

understanding, faculty of, 6, 14, 18–21, 47, 50, 53, 71, 76–77, 78, 82, 92, 94, 101, 103
uselessness, 79–81, 85n45. *See also* non-mastery

versatility, 20, 93, 103, 105. *See also* agility

Wang, Robin R., 68–69, 83n14, 84n18, 84n24
water: images and metaphors of, 66, 74–76, 92, 97, 100–101; wave-like movement of text, xvii, 82, 89–90, 94, 103, 104–105; River, Hudson, 92, 95. *See also* efficacy, dark; Flow Chart
wit, 19, 23, 46, 53, 54
writer: analytic, xii, xviiin4, 23, 31n52, 45, 97, 102; ironic, 18, 23, 49–50, 61, 80, 97, 103; synthetic, xii, xviiin4, 18, 45, 51, 102–103. *See also* genius; symphilosophie; writer, ironic
wu 無 ("non-presence"), 66, 66–67, 74, 84n18
wu wei ("inaction"), 62, 67, 68, 75, 79–80, 81. *See also* non-mastery

yang. *See* yin; yinyang
yin, 16, 69–70, 74–75, 78, 101. *See also* sage-ruler
yinyang, 16, 69–70, 72, 78, 84n24. *See also* yang; yin
you 有 ("presence"), 66, 67, 74, 84n18

Zhuangzi, 62–64, 70–71, 76, 85n45
Ziporyn, Brook, 63
ziran, 68, 74

ABOUT THE AUTHOR

Karolin Mirzakhan is lecturer of philosophy at Kennesaw State University (Atlanta, Georgia). She earned her PhD from DePaul University (Chicago, Illinois). Her doctoral research focused on the respective roles of comedy and irony in the philosophical projects of G. W. F. Hegel and Friedrich Schlegel. Her current writing projects are comparative in nature and take up Schlegelian irony in relationship with Daoism, Chicana feminism, and the contemporary American poet John Ashbery. She has two forthcoming chapters on Friedrich Schlegel: "Romantic Irony" and "Irony and the Possibility of Romantic Criticism: Friedrich Schlegel as Poet-Critic."

www.ingramcontent.com/pod-product-compliance
Lightning Source LLC
Chambersburg PA
CBHW050910300426
44111CB00010B/1458